Work and Leisure

Work and Leisure

A CONTEMPORARY SOCIAL PROBLEM

Edited by
ERWIN O. SMIGEL

COLLEGE AND UNIVERSITY PRESS
New Haven, Connecticut

To My Parents,
Joseph and Ida Smigel,
Whose Work is Their Leisure

Contents

ERWIN O. SMIGEL
New York University

Introduction

Hard facts about leisure are not easy to come by. Information concerning the interrelationship between work and leisure is even more difficult to find. Among the many reasons for this scarcity, possibly the most important is the Calvinist feeling in American culture that work alone is good—that a preoccupation with leisure borders on an endorsement of sin. Even in sociology one sometimes meets the attitude that the study of leisure is a concern with the trivial and the insignificant, that writers and researchers in this field are themselves engaged in leisure-time activity rather than in productive work.

Recently, however, this attitude began to undergo a change which in part reflects growing public concern about the work-leisure complex—a concern that grows out of fear of unemployment and has its roots in the 1929-39 depression, with its enforced "leisure." Automation, with its threat and promise of increased free time, has magnified the general awareness of the subject, and unions demands for a 35-hour week[1] have kept the discourse current. Sociological theories dealing with the dysfunctional use of free time are beginning to be discussed outside of academic walls, and one occasionally hears public comment on the proper and improper use of leisure time. The concern to date has focused on the behavior of special groups—for example, the juvenile delinquent who has dropped out of school, or the moonlighting unionman who has just had the hours of his primary job reduced.

The study of leisure, however, involves some unsolved problems. To help set the stage for the articles which appear in this collection, let us first look at the difficulties which stand in the way of researchers in this field;[2] and let us consider some of the problems which grow out of the potential of additional free time, as well as the difficulties of planning for it.

The researcher's first difficulty originates from the confusion over the meaning of the word leisure. A common error is that of using the term leisure when the use of leisure is actually being discussed. The confusion is compounded when words such as recreation, amusement, fun, pleasure, play, hobby, idleness, free time, and leisure are employed interchangeably. Two major schools of thought have emerged concerning the definition of leisure. The first is headed by political scientist and philosopher Sebastian de Grazia and drama critic Walter Kerr,[3] who champion the definition of the ancient Greeks. De Grazia offers, as the key to the meaning of leisure, "freedom from the necessity of being occupied,"[4] which paraphrases Aristotle. A poem published in the July 5, 1962, issue of *The Reporter* is a succinct statement of de Grazia's and Kerr's philosophic position on the proper use of leisure.

Time, Gentlemen, Please
Americans Found to Lack Leisure: Philosopher Says They Keep Too Busy During Time Spent Off the Job.

New York Times

Lie down and listen to the crabgrass grow,
The faucet leak, and learn to leave them so.
Feel how the breezes play about your hair
And sunlight settles on your breathing skin.
What else can matter but the drifting glance
On dragonfly or sudden shadow there
Of swans aloft and the whiffle of their wings
On air to other ponds? Nothing but this:
To see, to wonder, to receive, to feel
What lies in the circle of your singleness.
Think idly of a woman or a verse
Or bees or vapor trails or why the birds
Are still at noon. Yourself, be still—
There is no living when you're nagging time
And stunting every second with your will.
You work for this: to be the sovereign
Of what you slave to have—not
Slave.

—SEC

Nothing so poetic expresses the meaning of leisure for the members of the second school. By leisure, this group means free time, which is the meaning assigned to the term by most modern sociologists. This collection, then, might equally well have been called *Work and Free Time.* There is, nevertheless, some disagreement about what free time is. Is it merely time independent of work? If so, how is forced free time brought about by unemployment or unwanted retirement to be considered? Or must free time, in order to be considered leisure, be unobligated time or paid free time? Fortunately, the potential semantic confusions are usually avoided because each writer tends to define his terms.

Even if agreement were reached on a definition of leisure, actual study of the phenomenon remains complex: How leisure is used may differ with time, with class and occupation, as well as with nationality and religion; and how it is used affects how it is defined. What once might have been considered leisure need not be so considered today. School, for example, meant leisure to the ancient Greeks; today, for the majority in the United States, it does not. Compulsory mass education, with its utilitarian emphasis, has moved learning into the area of assigned responsibility—and thus, for most, it becomes work. One does not, however, have to go back to the ancient Greeks to show differences in the use of leisure time; a bulletin posted by a merchant for his employees in 1822 provides us with a picture, not only of "recommended" leisure pursuits but also of work requirements and amount of free time.

RULES FOR CLERKS[5]

1. This store must be opened at Sunrise. No mistake. Open 6 o'clock A.M. Summer and Winter. Close about 8:30 or 9 P.M. the year round.
2. Store must be swept—dusted—doors and windows opened—lamps filled, trimmed and chimneys cleaned—counters, base shelves and show cases dusted—pens made—a pail of water and also the coal must be brought in before breakfast, if there is time to do it and attend to all the customers who call.
3. The store is not to be opened on the Sabbath day unless absolutely necessary and then only for a few minutes.

4. Should the store be opened on Sunday, the clerks must go in alone and get tobacco for customers in need.
5. The clerk who is in the habit of smoking Spanish Cigars— being shaved at the barbers—going to dancing parties and other places of amusement and being out late at night—will assuredly give his employer reason to be ever suspicious of his integrity and honesty.
6. Clerks are allowed to smoke in the store provided they do not wait on women with a "stogie" in the mouth.
7. Each clerk must pay not less than $5.00 per year to the Church and must attend Sunday School regularly.
8. Men clerks are given one evening a week off for courting and two if they go to prayer meeting.
9. After the 14 hours in the store the leisure hours should be spent mostly in reading.

While the strict rules of the Protestant Ethic have not all disappeared, there are observable differences between modern norms and those listed above.

Leisure may also differ by social class, by occupation, and by life cycle. Harold L. Wilensky in this volume finds there is no longer a leisure class. In fact, individuals who in other days might have qualified for this category now work harder than many members of the working classes. We have included in this collection some examples of differences in styles of life for various social classes, but the differences do not occur only along the dimension of class. Joel E. Gerstl finds that members of the same class who are engaged in different occupations have somewhat different lesiure-time goals.

Certainly, broad differences between white collar and blue collar workers are evident. What data are available seem to indicate that persons in manual occupations spend much of their leisure time in physical pursuits and those in intellectual occupations spend a good deal of their free time in intellectual endeavors. When professors were asked by Gerstl how they would use a hypothetical two additional hours a day, 78 per cent thought they would read. In other words, as Bennett M. Berger points out, problems of leisure cannot be understood without knowledge of the groups that have the problem. This includes understanding how various groups feel about the work they are doing. Robert

Dubin, whose award-winning paper, "Industrial Workers' Worlds," appears in this volume, found that for workers, work was not a central life interest; while Louis H. Orzack discovered for professional people (nurses) that work was a central life interest. The information concerning the labor-leisure patterns of professional people indicates that the distinction between work and leisure is not always clear. Much of work for this group may be considered as leisure. This may change, however, as the distinctions between occupations and professions narrow.

The distinction between work and leisure may also become blurred for the individual—for example, the tennis player who turns professional or the rich man's son who plays at politics and is made chairman of a committee or is elected to office.

The very fact that society does not stand still makes research in the social sciences difficult. When an aircraft plant experimented with giving their employees a three-day weekend, Rolf Meyersohn had a unique opportunity to study both workers' attitudes toward a four-day week and their activities on that extra day. He interviewed workers in the plant at the beginning of the experiment and then again six months later. In the latter interviews, he found the situation radically changed because the country was in a recession and many of his original sample were laid off. Meyersohn was able to gather valuable information about the use of the extra day, and a bonus in that he has data on people before and during a recession. The study, however, could not be completed as planned.

Leisure is difficult to measure because much of it is intangible. If a man commutes to work, is the time he takes for travel to be considered work or free time? It may depend on the individual. If he looks forward to seeing his friends in the car pool, if he enjoys reading his paper on the train to the suburbs or the martini in the club car, one can argue that part of his trip, at least, is leisure. It is hard to measure subjective evaluations. To the extent that joy, happiness, and pleasure are involved in leisure, true assessment is difficult. Is sleeping leisure or is only a certain kind of sleep leisure? The problem of appraising the amount of available leisure is simplified if one arbitrarily labels all free time as leisure. But measuring its uses is a more subtle problem.

Many studies try to measure the use of leisure by estimating how much money is spent on recreation or how much time is spent watching television.

Edward Gross, in his contribution to this volume, while presenting one sociological way of looking at leisure and play, discusses their function. He notes, among other uses of leisure, that it may be recuperative, creative, or a boredom reliever. However, Robert J. Havighurst, in an article which appeared in the *American Journal of Sociology,* found that different kinds of leisure can have the same significance—the same use.[6] This makes it difficult always to know the function of a specific type of leisure activity. The problem is increased if personality has to be considered. Havighurst insists that it does.

In our society, work and leisure have always been interrelated. Automation and the possibility of additional free time have caused some concern about how this time will be used; how it will change society. One fear is that many people are not properly trained to know what to do with additional leisure time. Other problems arise involving changing work conditions and leisure. William A. Faunce discusses those most directly affected by automation. Berger, and Weiss and Riesman mention many others, and there is little need to anticipate them here. The problem of planning for leisure time, which worries Weiss and Riesman, involves most of the same difficulties encountered by researchers in the field. Perhaps the greatest handicap that besets planning stems from the value system, which frowns on society arranging for leisure, and from a lack of tradition of leisure which hinders creative thinking about leisure decision-making.

The appendix written by Peter Henle provides a concise and valuable overview of hours worked by individuals in the various industries, the extent of paid vacations and holidays, and the changes in the availability of free time. Many readers will find Henle's article a good starting point for their exposure to the problems of leisure.

Despite the many difficulties placed in the way of research and of planning for free time mentioned in this introduction and in this book, work on leisure continues, and this volume is but one example of what has been produced. Extensive bibliographies collected by Rolf Meyersohn,[7] and Reuel Denney and Mary Lea Meyersohn[8] provide a picture of the magnitude and breadth of the leisure field. Denney and Meyersohn found it necessary to divide their bibliography into twenty different categories. They discovered that information about the field of leisure came from seven different sources: market research; historical studies; surveys of planned and organized leisure sponsored by educators, social workers, and recreationists; the play movement; psychological research, including the media of mass communications; sociology and studies of the production and control aspects of mass media communications; and amusements themselves.[9]

The last few years have brought the publication of a number of books and special issues of journals. In 1958, Martin H. and E. S. Neumayer's revised text *Leisure and Recreation* reappeared. In that same year, Eric Larrabee and Rolf Meyersohn edited a comprehensive collection of articles entitled *Mass Leisure*. In 1960, Max Kaplan wrote a textbook *Leisure in America: A social Inquiry;* and Nels Anderson's text *Work and Leisure* also appeared in 1962. The most significant current volume on leisure published abroad[10] was written by Joffre Dumazedier in 1962, *Vers une Civilisation Du Loisir?* And in 1963 The Free Press will publish Harold L. Wilensky's book on work roles, career patterns, and leisure styles. His contribution to this collection suggests that Wilensky's volume is certain to make an important contribution to the analyses of work and leisure. *The American Journal of Sociology* (May, 1957), *International Social Science Journal* (1960), and *Social Problems* (Summer, 1961), among others, have brought out whole issues on leisure. Under the direction of David Riesman, the Center for the Study of Leisure has been a focal point for research. Some of the results of the Center's work have yet to appear. Rolf Meyersohn's contribution, published for the first time in this volume, had its origins in the Center. Other publications could be mentioned, but this list provides some idea of the extent of the field and the work that has recently been accomplished.

This publication represents only a fragment of what has been and still must be studied about the subject of work and leisure. Although most of the articles presented here have been written by sociologists for sociologists, the selections should certainly be of interest to the general public as well, or at least to that portion of it aware of and concerned about the possibly disruptive impact of sociological changes that will inevitably accompany the shifting work patterns in this increasingly automated industrial society.

Work and Leisure is sponsored by the Society for the Study of Social Problems, a nonprofit organization whose purpose, as its charter indicates, is to: "stimulate the application of scientific method and theory to the study of vital social problems, encourage problem-centered social research, and foster cooperative relations among persons and organizations engaged in the application of scientific sociological findings to the formulation of social policies." Four of the articles included here were first published under my editorship in *Social Problems,* the official journal of the society, in a special issue devoted to work and leisure. It is appropriate in light of this fact, and given the problem-solving interests of the society, that this volume be published under the auspices of The Society for the Study of Social Problems.

NOTES

1. The International Brotherhood of Electrical Workers, Local 3 recently won a battle for the 25-hour week.
2. Some of the problems discussed here are common to most sociological research.
3. Walter Kerr, *The Decline of Pleasure* (New York: Simon and Schuster, 1962).
4. Sebastian de Grazia, *Of Time, Work and Leisure* (New York: The Twentieth Century Fund, 1962), p. 14.
5. Quoted from Delbert C. Miller and William H. Form, *Industrial Sociology* (New York: Harper & Brothers, 1951), p. 561. They discovered it in "We and Our Business" (Carson, Pirie, Scott and Company, 1927), p. 20.
6. Robert J. Havighurst, "The Leisure Activities of the Middle-Aged," *American Journal of Sociology,* LXIII (September, 1957), 160.
7. Eric Larrabee and Rolf Meyersohn, eds., *Mass Leisure* (Glencoe, Ill.: The Free Press, 1958), pp. 389-419.
8. Reuel Denney and Mary Lea Meyersohn, "A Preliminary

Bibliography on Leisure," *American Journal of Sociology*, LXII (May, 1957), 602-15.

    9. Ibid., p. 602.

    10. Johan Huizinga's *Homo Ludens: A Study of the Play Element in Culture* (Boston: The Beacon Press, 1955) was published in German in 1944. It is the best known modern book from a foreign source written in the general area of leisure; in fact, it is regarded by many as a classic.

Work and Leisure

BENNETT M. BERGER

University of Illinois

1

The Sociology of Leisure:
Some Suggestions*

IN A WORLD FULL OF NEWSPAPERS whose headlines daily remind us of the continuing reign of misery and wretchedness in much of the world, and with the persistent cloud of nuclear war hanging over the heads even of the prosperous, the "problem" of leisure is one that we are distinctly privileged to have. Yet the study of leisure is not trivial—far from it. It is, however, worth noting at the outset that leisure assumes the status of a major problem only in a society which has been gripped by a "revolution of rising expectations." Unlike revolutions in underdeveloped countries, our revolution of rising expectations grows out of the demand for psychological as well as material benefits. An affluent society turns its attention to the pursuit of happiness; a well-fed society turns its attention to mental health; a successful society turns its attention to what Daniel Lerner[1] has called "comfort and fun," to personal "fulfillment," that elusive but supposed concomitant of success.

Despite the fact that "the problem of leisure" is already a conventional phrase in the language of the social sciences, the problem has hardly been formulated and the *concept* of leisure has only rarely been directly confronted.[2] To be sure, some problems of leisure may be understood without much attention

---

* Reprinted from *Industrial Relations,* Vol. 1, No. 2, February, 1962.

to the difficulties of conceptualization. Negroes who do not
have access to public parks, beaches, theaters, and so on, may
be said to have a leisure problem. Culturally deprived persons
whose backgrounds handicap them from participation in important voluntary associations, and who are hence deprived of
access to sources of power and influence, may also be said by
some to have a leisure problem. But these are not situations
which are typically referred to as problems of leisure. The
phrase, "problem of leisure," also evokes images of the aged
rocking in shabby rooms, poor, lonely, unattended, with little
to do but wait for death; of adolescents on slum street corners
answering with apparently senseless violence the anxious question of "what'll we do tonight?"; of large blocs of a nation's
population sitting each evening in darkened living rooms lit
only by that blue light from which emanates the irrelevant
shadows which people the imaginative life of a society. These
images, and the facts which underlie them, are at the core of
the concern expressed over the disposition of free time.

Nevertheless, it seems to me that little is contributed to the
understanding of these particular problems by conceiving them
as problems of leisure. The aged, certainly, have special
problems, some of them imposed by sudden retirement, some
by the infirmities of age, still others by the breakup of families.
Basically, however, these are problems of the aged and can be
understood without invoking the unexamined abstraction, leisure.
Similarly, problems of adolescents have been intensified or
dramatized in recent years by, among other things, their increasingly late entrance into the labor market, by their increasingly early admittance into adolescent status, and by the sight
of Negro, Puerto Rican, and other slum youth who are doomed,
amid the general prosperity, to an environment of urban blight.

The problems of mass leisure (perhaps best symbolized by
the TV narcotic) are inextricably bound up with a technology
which renders work progressively more routinized and "easier"
(though perhaps not less exhausting), with the purchasing power
of large masses of people in the "culture market," and with the
consequent rise of enormous "culture industries." In short, each
problem of leisure is almost impossible to formulate or to solve

without understanding the position of the groups who *have* the problem and the nature of the social and economic changes underlying their problems. More people are presented with more time at various stages of the life cycle than ever before— time when they are free to seek the inner satisfactions which we seem legitimately to expect from leisure. It adds little to our understanding of the difficulties of specific groups to perceive these difficulties as problems of leisure, unless this approach provides clues to aspects of the problem that were previously hidden and aids in the development of a theory of leisure.

Two Traditions in the Discussion of Leisure

Problems are not self-evident. Thus we may raise the empirical question of *to* whom and *for* whom leisure is a problem —for not everybody is concerned about the leisure problems of everybody else. The more familiar social problems of leisure have developed out of the concern *by* specific groups *for* the leisure of other specific groups, and an examination of these groups may cast some light on the conceptual problem of leisure.

Whose leisure is usually a public concern? Certain salient groups may be identified: the aged, children, youth, the unemployed, the handicapped, the ill, and inmates in prisons and mental institutions are groups that come immediately to mind.[3] In general, these groups are relatively unproductive categories of the population; they also often lack many of the basic institutional connections which bind individuals to society. Perhaps most important of all their common characteristics is their vulnerability to public action: in one way or another, these groups tend to be composed of less than fully competent persons. They are dependent, and by virtue of their dependence the disposition of their free time becomes a legitimate concern of those who are responsible for them. Who is responsible, who concerned? The groups seem to be composed primarily of civic officials, certain categories of group workers and social workers, some teachers, clergymen, and people at least to some extent vocationally concerned with the welfare of others. The social problem of leisure in this context seems to be one of providing the dependent groups (to the extent that they are unable to provide for themselves) with opportunities for "wholesome" activities. By keeping them busy and productive and by engaging them in social relations, these activities are expected to give meaning to lives otherwise subject to unusually severe stresses.

The leisure of the masses also gives rise to a good deal of publicly expressed concern. This concern, however, is not typically expressed by the groups I have cited above, but rather by intellectuals or cultural elites, whose concern over mass leisure seems to reflect their fear of the power of the masses in the culture market and the consequent threat to the traditional values of high culture. There are two major ideological approaches to this problem. Conservative intellectuals tend to be pessimistic about the possibilities of elevating popular taste on a mass scale and consequently see the social stratification of culture as inevitable. In their view, cultural elites should tend the garden of high culture and ignore the mass media which, after all, reflect the tastes of the markets they serve.

Liberal and radical intellectuals, on the other hand, tend to accuse the suppliers of mass culture of catering to the lowest levels of popular taste in order to achieve the highest of net profit.[4] These intellectuals confer upon the mass media an enormous potential for elevating popular taste, a potential which they argue is not only rarely used but is actually perverted by the commitment of the media to diversion, entertainment, and escape. In other words, they consider the media committed to serve as a distraction from, and compensation for, the presumably drab and monotonous routines of the working lives of the masses. Richard Hoggart, in his description of the decline of English working-class culture, gives precise expression to this view when he says, "The strongest objection to the more trivial popular entertainments is not that they prevent their [consumers] . . . from becoming highbrow, but that they make it harder for people without an intellectual bent to become wise in their own way."[5]

These two types of concern about leisure—that is, the concern of intellectuals and elites over popular taste and mass culture and the concern of more-or-less professional "do-gooders" over the "wholesome" disposition of the free time of relatively vulnerable, dependent groups—are contemporary instances of traditional approaches to leisure which go back a long way and have only rarely complemented one another. One tradition, probably dating from the relatively early stages of industrialization in the West, conceives of leisure as "free time" or time not devoted to paid occupations; leisure activities are viewed primarily as re-creative and restorative; historically the problems involved are associated with the poor, the dependent, or the laboring classes. The much older, classical tradition conceives of leisure in the Greek sense, as "schooling" or cultivation of the self, as a preoccupation with the values of high culture. Historically this tradition has been associated with the functions of aristocratic, patrician, or leisure classes, since other classes were not culturally important.

To the Greeks, leisure was concerned with those activities that were worthy of a free man, activities we might today call "culture." Politics, debate, philosophy, art, ritual, and athletic contests were activities worthy of a free man because they expressed the moral core of a style of life. Their nobility was not, ideally, compromised or diluted by mere instrumental or productive purposes. "Work" as instrumental or productive activity was regarded as below the dignity of a free man, fit only for slaves and women. Leisure, in this aristocratic usage, is concerned with the maintenance of a style of life expressing the highest values of a culture. There is no problem of leisure because those who have it are bred to it.

What may be called the Protestant or industrial view of leisure is something quite different. When Calvinism sanctified work and industrialism ennobled it, what followed was the separation of work and leisure, the emphasis of economically productive functions as the most significant aspect of life, and the relegation of leisure to the status of spare time—time especially vulnerable to the ministrations of the Devil (witness the depravity of the poor) unless it were used productively to restore or refresh the organism for its primary purpose, work, or for unambiguously "wholesome" purposes such as prayer, Bible reading, or the disciplining of children. With the onset

of industrialism, the functions of creating and maintaining the
aristocratic values—formerly the avocations of gentlemen of
leisure or the preoccupations of men of talent kept as ornaments
by aristocratic families or subsidized by the state—were increasingly taken over by occupational groups whose services
were paid for through the market economy.

This brief review of the two traditions of leisure should
suggest, above all, that a concept of leisure must be normative.
To neither tradition, however different their evaluations of it,
is leisure merely neutral time involving neutral activities. For
Aristotle, leisure was the aim of life; for the Calvinist divine, it
represented a threat to the Protestant virtues. In either case,
classical aristocrat or Protestant preacher, both had clear ideas
about the activities to which this time was to be devoted.
Where the viability of the Greek idea of leisure rested on slave
labor, the Protestant deification of work was supported by the
sin of idleness (which to the Greeks was a virtue). The meanings
of work and leisure are inextricably related both to each other
and to the cultural norms which define their moral place in a
social order. A sociological definition which ignores this fact
does so at the peril of becoming irrelevant.

Toward a Normative Concept of Leisure

Is there a way of marrying these normative traditions and
their associated concerns, thereby creating a unified, value-
relevant approach to the sociology of leisure? To some extent,
economic development and the spread of political democracy
have answered this question for us by bringing the masses onto
the stage of history. At the same time, the more severe and
ascetic features of Puritanism have been discredited. As citizens,
the masses have had human rights and secular dignity conferred
on them; as free men they have been invited to participate in
"activities worthy of a free man," to pursue happiness and
personal fulfillment. And as possessors of discretionary income
they have acquired the means to make these goals more than
mere formal possibilities.

At the same time, the modern world has witnessed the near
disappearance of a leisure class in the classical sense of an

aristocratic group with time completely free of the need to labor productively. Today, practically all of us work and practically all of us have some "free time" beyond the minimum needed to restore or refresh the body for its economic tasks. We are all, at least in principle, compromised Greek citizens carrying the burden of compromised Protestant ethics. The industrial system has created hundreds of thousands of jobs that we feel are degrading,[6] but we are unwilling to do without the wealth which the system creates. We no longer feel that idleness is sinful, but we still retain something of the expectation that work should have moral content and feel rather cheated and slightly betrayed when we discover that moral content has simply disappeared from much industrial work.

It is out of such ambiguous situations that sociologies are made. One would expect a burgeoning sociology of leisure. This is not the case, however. We know a great deal about what people do with their free time, but only a small part of this knowledge has been gathered by students who have undertaken a conscious investigation of leisure. We know, for example, a considerable amount about who participates in what kinds of voluntary associations with what frequency, but the scholars who have done the work do not typically think of themselves as students of leisure. Kinsey studying sex is surely studying leisure. And something like this can be said about studies of mass media impact, juvenile delinquency, family life, and many other fields.[7] Moreover, it seems to me that less has been contributed to a sociological understanding of leisure by studies consciously directed to that end than by good community studies which are only incidentally or peripherally concerned with it. Although books like *Street Corner Society, Elmtown's Youth, Democracy in Jonesville, Middletown, Deep South, Crestwood Heights,* and many others, do not typically deal with the conceptual problem of leisure, they contain not only a wealth of data on free-time activities but data made meaningful through their linkage to a theory of community or class or subculture or whatever the dominant focus of the book in question happens to be.

This theoretical relevance is precisely what is missing from

most of the contemporary empirical work in the sociology of
leisure. The sociology of leisure today is little else than a
reporting of survey data on what selected samples of individuals
do with the time in which they are not working and the correlation of these data with conventional demographic variables.[8]
There are several important exceptions to this general statement,
but they do not alter the melancholy fact that empirical proof
that rich people play polo more often than poor people gives
us little reason to hope that an incipient sociology of leisure is
taking shape. No genuine sociology of leisure is likely to emerge
until a body of data is reinforced by a theory of leisure—at the
very least by a conceptual understanding of what leisure is.

Leisure has been difficult to conceptualize for two very basic
reasons.[9] First, conceptualization in sociology requires the abstraction of a common property or properties from a relatively
wide range of events or social behavior. Leisure activities include
such a colossally varied assortment of behavior (everything from,
say, attendance at the President's Inaugural Ball to—as Louis
Kronenberger pointed out—wandering up and down railroad
yards collecting the names of Pullman cars and noting them
down in a little book) that it has been virtually impossible to
conceptualize it on a behavioral basis. Instead, a circumstance
of that behavior (that it goes on in time not given over to
paid occupations) has typically been made the sole criterion of
leisure. Such a definition tells us nothing about the normative
content of leisure, nor does it even invite questions about it;
it characterizes only the time in which leisure activities occur.
Strictly understood, the conventional opposition of work and
leisure is a false opposition because these terms characterize
different orders of phenomena: leisure is a kind of time, whereas
work is a kind of action. Students of leisure, however, do not
study time, they study behavior. To contrast work and leisure—
and we must contrast them, since they have sociological meaning
only vis-à-vis each other—we must conceive of leisure also as a
kind of action which, however, is distinguished from work.

The apparently simple characterization of leisure as free time
(two of the most complicated words in the language) or unobligated time seems to lead to precisely this kind of distinction:

the "free" of free time suggests that leisure activity is voluntary whereas work is constrained. This distinction brings us to the second difficulty with the conceptualization of leisure, because the very idea of free time belongs to a presociological age. If sociology has taught us anything it has taught us that no time is free of normative constraints; what is work for some, is leisure for others, it is said, and of course this is right. Is work work if I love it? Is leisure leisure if I feel it is burdensome or boring? These are the kinds of questions which make students of leisure tear their hair and in despair reach for the operational definition. Any normative distinction between work and leisure as action should be a distinction between the kinds of norms which constrain them or a distinction regarding the extent to which norms have been internalized.

If, sociologically speaking, no time is unconstrained, how can we save leisure as free time from the status of a sociological myth? One way is to invoke Kenneth Burke's famous phrase, "perspective by incongruity," and argue that leisure refers precisely to those activities (or nonactivities) that are *most* constrained by moral norms. Norms may exercise moral force because they are functionally complete (genuine virtue is, after all, its own reward). Or, in some cases, they may have been so thoroughly internalized—so much a matter of conscience and so little a matter of something objectively "out there"—that they are felt as motives or desires freely chosen or as moral responsibilities freely accepted.

This is a way of saying that leisure refers to those activities whose normative content renders them most important to us, those things that we want to do for their own sake or those things that we feel ethically (as distinguished from expediently) constrained to do.[10] *That these activities may empirically be found to occur most frequently in time not devoted to paid occupations is significant primarily as an indication that work has lost much of its moral content*—that work, which was once a calling from God to an earthly place, has become "a job": "it's a living."

This conception of work-leisure is normative. Transcending the usual distinction between work and leisure, it represents a comprehensive cultural ideal; it is, in short, an "ideal type" only imperfectly realized in the actual experience of individuals. At the same time, it is not a moralistic idea; it does not preach the gospel of leisure; it does not regard leisure as an unambiguous good under all circumstances. It is quite probable that certain social functions require predominantly instrumental or expedient motivation; the performance of some essential roles may very well be obstructed by deep moral commitments. But this view of leisure gives us the beginning of a normative concept which can be useful because it invites questions about the conditions under which this comprehensive ideal is attained or approximated, although it does erase the usual distinction between work and leisure.

In place of this distinction, the conception makes possible further distinctions between leisure and such associated terms as rest, relaxation, or recreation, which may not have much moral content; and by suggesting that not everything that one encounters in one's free time qualifies as leisure, it frees the concept from its operational identification with specific forms of, for example, games. But even if the study of leisure turns out to be primarily the study of fun and games, reading and gardening, hunting and fishing, watching and hearing (as I hope it does not), this still suggests only that we are looking away from work, occupations, and careers to find what morally involves the members of our society.

Alienation from Work and the Problem of Leisure

It is perhaps an indication of how far we have come from the great days of the Protestant Ethic that the very characterization of leisure as free time contains a damning judgment on work, for it suggests that what is not leisure is not free, that is, it is for slaves—which is precisely as the Greeks would have had it. But this judgment is a disappointed one because we have not completely lost the expectation that we have some right to moral satisfaction in work; the Protestant Ethic dies hard—values always do—and leaves in us a lingering sense of betrayal when work seems meaningless.

Where work is concerned with wresting food from the earth, creating warmth and shelter for one's family, or even where, in societies undergoing industrialization, it is ideologically envisioned as the collective creation of a bright future (as it is today, for example, in the USSR and China), Protestant ethics have been eminently qualified to confer on such activities profound moral content. But where work is concerned with the manufacture of hoola hoops or mink coats for dogs or refrigerators that never need defrosting or automobiles that almost never need lubrication, and where men trained in English language and literature devote their worklives to the skillful use of the incomplete comparison in order to sell goods, even so versatile an instrument as our traditional value system learns its limitations.[11]

Lest I be misunderstood, I should make it clear that social criticism is not my intent here. The problem of leisure is not created merely by the growth of discretionary income, the reduction in the workweek, the pensioned retirement, and the lengthening span of life, just as alienation in work is not created primarily by the inherent properties of certain jobs.[12] Both problems are created when a value system is rendered apparently incapable of conferring honor on the typical situations which a social system engenders. Where inconsistencies exist between what the social system requires and what the value system prescribes, social problems are created, prominent among which are alienation from work and the problem of leisure, reverse sides of the same coin.

The social system, for example, has created longer adolescence, more years in retirement, and assembly-line jobs, but our value system contains no moral rhetoric with which to confer honor on these phenomena; the 21-year-old college boy is still something considerably less than a man, the aged in impoverished retirement are objects of pity or patronization, and the automobile assembly-line worker is every intellectual's model of alienation from work. Our social system needs and produces "organization men," but the words remain offensive to us; we are all status seekers, but nobody defends status seeking. We

don't know how: our value system does not provide us with
the moral vocabulary to defend much of the behavior and
many of the roles which the social structure requires.

In this respect, the Soviet countries have a bitter lesson to
teach us. Soviet cultural rhetoric is offensive to the ears of
Western intellectuals because it transparently and grossly attempts to confer moral significance on, and to create heroic
images of, precisely those roles and behavior to which the
Soviet social system is committed, images which to us are
sometimes laughable. The muscled worker raising his sledge-
hammer above the rubble, the Stakhanovite overproducing his
quota, the stocky, fresh-complexioned girl on the tractor, are
proper topics for heroic treatment and glorious characterization.
The collectivized Horatio Alger morality of Soviet rhetoric
confers heroic status on those types of individuals and roles that
actually represent the collective purposes of the state.

Consider the strain on our moral vocabulary if it were asked
to produce heroic myths of accountants, computer programmers,
and personnel executives. We prefer cowboys, detectives, bull
fighters, and sports-car racers, because these types embody the
virtues which our moral vocabulary is equipped to celebrate:
individual achievement, exploits, and prowess. Again, I should
make clear that this is *not* a criticism of what we have become
and certainly not a celebration of the harmony between Soviet
society and culture; it is, rather, an analysis of why we are
uneasy about what we have become. A culture which has not
learned to honor what it is actually committed to produce
creates an uneasy population.[13]

The problems of leisure and of alienation in work, then, are
problems created by the inconsistencies between normative
and social systems. Two adaptive responses to these problems
are typical. The more common response, where certain jobs are
not honored, is to withdraw emotion from work, to accept work
as something one has to do in order to make possible the things
one really cares about. Though the Protestant Ethic is by no
means in its grave, there is clearly a growing consensus (more
apparent, of course, on the lower levels of the occupational
ladder than on the higher) that the major moral satisfactions in

life are to be sought through leisure, not work. Or, in my own terms, leisure is to be sought through activities unconnected with occupations. The withdrawal of motivation may thus be replaced, for workers, by emotional involvement in the bowling league, the bridge club, the philatelist society, the golf score, the sports-car rally, or various kinds of spectator activities. For adolescents, there is "youth culture"; for the elderly, Golden Age Clubs.

Another kind of adaptation to alienation from work is much subtler. Manual workers can cope with alienation on the job by the invention of all sorts of factory games and status play. On professional and executive levels, one notes a surprising degree of sophisticated candor about alienation. It is, of course, true that job satisfaction studies[14] generally reveal that professionals and executives are much more satisfied with their jobs than factory workers, but "job satisfaction" does not necessarily tell us much about alienation. In several professional and executive milieux it has become fashionable, almost de rigueur, to be cynical about one's work. The point is that the sophistication and the subtlety of one's cynicism can be highly rewarding, thus creating a situation in which one can be quite alienated from work but quite satisfied with one's job.

The metaphor of the "rat race," so common in highly competitive occupations, suggests that work on higher occupational levels is hardly a sanctified, self-justifying thing. Even in academic life, that former citadel of self-justifying work, the phrase "publish or perish" and the utter cynicism with which scholars (frequently successful ones) typically speak of the mysterious science of grant-getting bear testimony not only to an incipient alienation from work but also to new patterns of sophisticated disaffection, the elegance of which may be granted considerable honor. For these folkways are frequently models of duplicity; functionally, they constitute the conversational equipment to deal with the psychological dimensions of success and failure. The successful contestant in a "rat race" may be all the more highly admired for his success, given the arduous nature of the competition. Thus when successful men characterize their occupational milieu as a "rat race," the characterization may well contain the not-too-well-hidden motive of self-congratulation. When, on the other hand, the characterization is made by the unsuccessful, the metaphor of the "rat race" functions as a "cooling" device;[15] it renders failure honorable, for losing in a race of four-legged rodents is testimony to one's two-legged humanity. To be sure, norms are operating here, and they may account in large part for much of the job satisfaction on higher levels, but these norms bear little resemblance to what we have in mind when we speak of our value system. Sociologists refer to such milieux as "deviant subcultures," and effective participation in them is in itself evidence of one's alienation from the dominant value system as applied to work.

In either case, whether it is the relatively simple alienation so characteristic of assembly-line work in factories or the highly sophisticated kind of alienation we find in the folkways of higher occupations, one thing is clear: the disengagement of self from occupational role not only is more common than it once was but is increasingly regarded as *proper*. Alienation would seem almost complete when one can say with honesty and moral conviction, "I am not what I do; do not judge me by what I do for a living," and when one turns to nonworking life for values and identity.

It may be objected that this analysis ignores important counter-tendencies in the nature and organization of work. Some cause for optimism regarding the problem of alienation has been sought, for example, in the fact that, of all occupational categories, highly skilled professional and technical occupations show the highest rates of growth. And since job satisfaction tends to be highest in the highly skilled manual classifications and in the nonmanual professional and technical classifications, the future should look somewhat brighter.

While there is clearly some basis for optimism in these occupational trends, there are at the same time several factors latent in them which should considerably temper that optimism. On blue-collar levels, for example, the newest automated types of skills are frequently the kind for which no readily available standards of approbation exist within the peer groups of skilled workers. The skills of a maintenance man in an automated plant, for example, are not the manual skills traditionally accorded honor by blue-collar workers. Moreover, to the extent that progressive refinements in the division of labor represent ever greater specialization of functions, occupational skills tend to become what Wilensky has called "status-invisible": "Ask a 'hindleg toenail remover' what he does and he will tell you he works at Swift's . . . the white-collar 'console operator,' too, will name the company, [but] not the job, because nobody has heard of this latest example of automation."[16] Where such conditions exist, the tendency of highly skilled jobs to command the moral identity of men is compromised; personal ties to work are weakened, and the relevance of working life to nonworking life is obscured.

Regarding professional occupations, bureaucratic organization continues increasingly to define the conditions of professional work. These conditions render such work less and less akin to the traditional model of the liberal professions, with their emphasis on responsibility, personal service, and creativity, and more and more akin to the bureaucratic model of professional and managerial skills organized in a "functionally rational" manner—a type of organization to which traditional professional norms can only be applied with great difficulty. To the extent that such skills can be routinized, managers and professionals, as Wilensky and others have noted, are themselves increasingly subject to "Taylorization," which tends to weaken further a moral commitment to work. Witness the complex, rather panicky response of many teachers to the prospect of automatic teaching devices. There are, of course, professional and technical milieux which are relatively insulated from these tendencies, but to the extent that work is subject to rationalization these will decrease, and unless norms can be found within our value system to celebrate bureaucratization, the withdrawal of motivation and the disengagement of self from work is likely to continue.

As work loses its power to command the moral identifications and loyalties of men, as men look away from work to find moral experience, society loses an important source of normative integration. Widespread belief in the inherent value of work gives economic institutions the power to perform certain necessary integrative functions, and the withdrawal of motivation from work seriously strains the network of bonds which relate the world of work to the world of non-work, and the individual to both.

In such a situation we may expect, if the functionalist view of society as a self-balancing system has any merit, the transfer of functions formerly performed by the institutions of work to the "leisure institutions," and this, it seems to me, is precisely the significance of the enormous increase in attention which the problem of leisure has received in recent years.[17] In much the same sense that functions formerly performed by the family and the church are increasingly shifted to the schools, reluctant and in many respects ill-equipped to handle them, "free time" is increasingly burdened with moral functions formerly performed by the institutions of work. Where public concern over leisure is not merely an attempt by moralistic busybodies to impose their own ideas of "wholesome" use of time on others, and where it is not professional or semi-professional mourning over the vulgarity of mass culture, it is a concern with the sources of moral solidarity. For with the weakening of the moral link which binds men to the institutions of work—and religion too—the major institutional sources of social cohesion become problematic.

The Task of a Sociology of Leisure

To my mind, the problem of leisure is a problem of finding, in the norms which exercise constraint in specific situations, the values which command moral identity and assent. The frequent appeals to individuals to use leisure "creatively" and to participate in local community institutions and voluntary associations are not likely to aid much in the solution of the problem because they beg the important questions of whether these activities actually do have moral force and whether the social structure actually does provide access to the goals which the culture recommends. Many of the recommended solutions to the problem of leisure, in short, would be viable only if there were no problem of leisure to begin with. The problem of leisure is exacerbated when men are asked to use their free time for activities beyond their means or for activities whose value they do not recognize.

The problem of leisure is difficult to treat intelligently because it lies in an area that is not amenable to our genius for organized solutions. The problem is a poignant one in a democratic industrial society because it is a Frankenstein's monster: it confronts the society with the spectre of an enormous amount of free time which is created by the society, but over which the society admits that it should, in principle, have little or no conscious influence or control. If leisure is time free of merely instrumental obligations, it is not subject to the criteria of efficiency and hence is immune to the power of rationality and organization. And if the great gift of unbeholden time and discretionary income creates a leisure whose dominant motifs are boredom, violence, and escape, the monster turns on its creator and challenges the viability of the democratic ideal.[18]

But if the values sought through leisure are difficult to find because of changes in the nature and organization of work and the receding horizons of aspiration, they are nevertheless there, both in traditional and in new forms, which is only to say that men have culture. The task of a sociology of leisure is to discover what these values are, the patterns of activity through which they are sought, and the features of social structure which tend to change or sustain them.[19] The sociology of leisure is that part of the sociology of culture which attempts to discover the moral character of a style of life by studying the behavior of groups under conditions where that behavior is least constrained by exclusively instrumental considerations. Increasingly, these conditions are found outside of occupations, and where they are, the "problem" is not too *much* time and money, but too *little*. Leisure styles are created by the kinds of leisure activities that, empirically, tend to cluster together; these are not random, and the sociological analysis of them is the study of how social structure facilitates or obstructs the efforts of men to find in their freest time the moral satisfactions which value systems must provide.

NOTES

1. See Daniel Lerner, "Comfort and Fun: Morality in a Nice Society," *American Scholar*, XXVII (Spring, 1958), 153-65.

2. The classic confrontation is, of course, Johan Huizinga, *Homo Ludens: The Play Element in Culture* (London: Routledge & Paul, 1949). For a Catholic view, see Joseph Pieper, *Leisure, the Basis of Culture* (New York: Pantheon Books, 1952). Though the word "leisure" is hardly mentioned in it, Werner Jaeger's *Paideia: The Ideals of Greek Culture* (New York: Oxford University Press, 1943), is probably the best single source for a classical understanding of leisure. Clement Greenberg, "Work and Leisure Under Industrialism," *Commentary*, XVI (July, 1953), 54-63, is a thoughtful consideration of the impact of industrialization on traditional views of leisure. None of these writings, however, are by sociologists. Almost any of David Riesman's several essays on work and leisure are very helpful in the study of leisure, and Max Kaplan makes a heroic but unsuccessful attempt to conceptualize leisure sociologically in *Leisure in America: A Social Inquiry* (New York: Wiley, 1960), Chap. 2. The most promising current work is that outlined by Harold Wilensky in "Work, Careers, and Social Integration," *International Social Science Journal*, XII (Fall, 1960), 543-60.

3. But not *all* members of these groups. The leisure of rich and prominent aged persons seems not to be a legitimate concern of others. A public or private attempt to help Dwight Eisenhower, Herbert Hoover, Bernard Baruch, or Douglas MacArthur to spend their declining years more "productively" or satisfyingly would probably be regarded as presumptuous.

4. Bernard Rosenberg and David Manning White, eds., *Mass Culture* (Glencoe, Ill.: Free Press, 1957), contains several examples of both views. For an especially good example of the conservative view, see Edward Shils, "Daydreams and Nightmares: Reflections on the Criticism of Mass Culture," *Sewanee Review*, LXV (Autumn, 1957), 587-608.

5. *The Uses of Literacy* (London: Chatto and Windus, 1957), p. 276.

6. Degrading, that is, in terms of the values created by industrialism and which define what men have a legitimate right to expect.

7. This is typical of the way fields of specialization develop in sociology and, perhaps, in other disciplines too: not because of a rigorously logical division of labor, but rather because of historical accidents in which specific "claims" are laid to certain kinds of data. Sociology's traditional interests in the family and in various aspects of "social disorganization" are due in large measure to the fact that these "fields" had not been claimed by other disciplines at the time sociology formally developed.

8. Wed to an operational definition of leisure as time not spent in gainful employment, such studies can only rarely get beyond the level of empirical generalization implicit in simple correlation. Studies of leisure and stratification are good cases in point. See, for example, R. Clyde White, "Social Class Differences in the Use of Leisure," *American Journal of Sociology*, LXI (September, 1955), 145-50; Alfred C. Clarke, "Leisure and Occupational Prestige," *American Sociological Review*, XXI (June, 1956), 301-7; Leonard Reissman, "Class, Leisure, and Social Participation," *American Sociological Review*, XIX (February, 1954), 76-84. Saxon Graham correlates the data from his study with both class and rural-urban residence. See Chapter XVIII of his *American Culture* (New York: Harper, 1957). Marjorie Donald and Robert Havighurst relate variations in the meanings attached to leisure to certain demographic variables. See "The Meanings of Leisure," *Social Forces*, XXXVII (May, 1959), 355-60.

9. That it *is* difficult to conceptualize is implicit in the failure of one recent symposium to come to any agreement on what the term means. See the introductory remarks in Robert W. Kleemeier, ed., *Aging and Leisure* (New York: Oxford University Press, 1961), p. 4. This book is probably the best of the several collections published in recent years on the problems contained in its title, but its utility extends beyond the problems of the aged. Sebastian de Grazia's contribution, "The Uses of Time," presents an enormous amount of data collected for studies under the Twentieth Century Fund; Nelson Foote's chapter, "Methods for the Study of Meaning in Use of Time," carefully reviews the several techniques of data collection in leisure studies. See, in addition, the contributions of Meyersohn, Wilensky, and Gordon.

10. That one finds it emotionally more difficult to beg off (for phony reasons) from a previously accepted invitation to a party given by a friend, than to call the boss to say one's sick and not coming to work, suggests that leisure obligations are *more* thoroughly internalized than obligations to work. Where this is true (and, of course, it is not under all circumstances), it suggests that free time is *more* obligated precisely because it is "free"; where commitments are voluntary they carry with them a felt responsibility.

11. Advertising, of course, is the great bête noire of social critics, the very model of organized cynicism. What an interesting study of reactions might be obtained if the writers of pamphlets which are published by the big advertising agencies for distribution to college majors in English and journalism and which describe the satisfactions to be achieved through careers in advertising were confronted with the novels, stories, and nonfiction written by ex-advertising men about life along James Madison's avenue!

12. See the following three articles which document the increases

in leisure time and the money spent on leisure pursuits: Joseph
Zeisel, "The Workweek in American Industry, 1850-1956"; Seymour
Wolfbein, "The Changing Length of Working Life"; and "30 Billion
for Fun," by the editors of *Fortune*. All three articles are reprinted in
Eric Larrabee and Rolf Meyersohn, editors, *Mass Leisure* (Glencoe,
Ill.: Free Press, 1958). See also, Sebastian de Grazia, "Tomorrow's
Good Life," *Teacher's College Record*, LXI, April, 1960, for an
argument regarding why such statistics may be misleading; and
Ida Craven, "Leisure," in Larrabee and Meyersohn, *op. cit.*, and
Harold Wilensky, "The Uneven Distribution of Leisure," *Social
Problems*, IX, Summer, 1961, for evidence on the large number of
holy days and feast days in the ancient and medieval worlds.

13. The plethora of television heroes who bear no relation to
anyone in real life may not be due to the cynicism of sponsors and
network executives. Such people might be only too pleased to present
dramatic shows about accountants, IBM technicians, and junior
executives, if only writers knew how to write them.

14. See the very able summary and analysis of these studies by
Robert Blauner, "Work Satisfaction and Industrial Trends in Modern
Society," in Walter Galenson and Seymour M. Lipset, eds., *Labor
and Trade Unionism* (New York: Wiley, 1960).

15. The expert here is Erving Goffman, "Cooling the Mark Out:
Some Aspects of Adaptation to Failure," *Psychiatry*, XV (November,
1952), 451-63.

16. Harold Wilensky, "Work, Careers . . . ," p. 19. On the ambig-
uous status of automated skills, see Robert Blauner, *Freedom in
Work and the Diversity of Industrial Environments* (unpublished
Ph.D. dissertation, University of California, 1961), Chap. V.

17. Edward Gross assures us that leisure performs important
functions in solving all four of the "system problems" of Parsons and
his collaborators, but he does not suggest why this discovery was not
made until very recently. See Edward Gross, "A Functional Approach
to Leisure Analysis," *Social Problems*, IX, Summer, 1961. This issue
of *Social Problems* is wholly devoted to articles on leisure.

18. The great success of the motion picture *Marty*—with its
recurrent refrain of "what'll we do tonight?"—suggests the dramatic
appeal of the attempt to overcome ennui. Having no ready answer
to the question of "what'll we do tonight?" provokes great anxiety
because having "nothing to do" is cause for shame in a society
burdened by the old view that idleness is vice and the new view that
great demands on one's time are evidence of high estate.

19. What, for example, is it about our social structure that accounts for the transformation of the bowling alley from a haunt of
thieves, murderers, and con men, into an eminently respectable
place to take the family for an evening of wholesome fun, whereas
the poolroom has been unable to lose its unsavory reputation?

EDWARD GROSS

University of Minnesota

2

A Functional Approach to Leisure Analysis*

THE PROBLEMS FACED in studying leisure are both consequence and cause of the problems faced in studying work, for one is usually defined as the absence of or preparation for the other. If work is what a man does when he would rather be doing something else, then leisure is what he does when he does not have to work. Since work arises from the need to supply the maintenance-needs—food, clothes, shelter—and since these are obviously necessary to survival, work has associated with it an inevitable quality and necessary irksomeness. Man, an animal after all, must, in Piaget's sense,[1] accommodate himself to the facts of brute existence. Leisure refers to free time, free, that is, from the need to be concerned about maintenance, a freedom that could be purchased with slaves by a leisure class, or with money earned through labor by the working population. And, as Margaret Mead[2] notes, it *is* usually earned or at least deserved. Work gives one not only the means but also the right to free time, an attitude which is a legacy, she feels, from Puritanism. Such an attitude is contrasted with that in ancient, Western civilizations, where leisure was felt to be the goal and proper activity of the whole man. Work was degrading, in a class with bodily excretion, necessary, but only in the sense of an enabling

---

* Reprinted from *Social Problems,* Vol. 9, No. 1, Summer, 1961.

utility or facility, a meaning close, paradoxically, to that of recreation in modern times.

Yet though work certainly does have, as Don Martindale notes,[3] instrumental value, and play has intrinsic value, work can *become* play in a genuine sense. Simmel[4] saw play arising when forms became ends in themselves: hunting for food evolved into The Fox Hunt, a phenomenon often leading, in turn, as Gregory Stone[5] notes, to the spectacle in which play becomes the life-work of the players. More generally, work goes beyond the provision of the mere necessaries of life. "It is not physical hunger," writes Daniel Bell, "which is the driving force; there is a new hunger. The candied carrot, the desire for goods, has replaced the stick; the standard of living has become a built-in automatic drive."[6]

Such a claim forces us to look again at the conception of leisure as noncompulsive, a conception often expressed as follows. *Fortune* magazine in describing precisely the economic aspects of leisure defines it as an activity "undertaken by choice, not by necessity."[7] Johan Huizinga[8] conceives of play as "never a task" and Gregory Stone and Marvin Taves follow him in describing it as "superfluous in character, a disinterested, extraordinary and 'unreal' activity. . . . Play in its pure form, stands apart from work."[9] The contrast of play or leisure with work in this sense was never dramatized more clearly than in Jeremy Bentham's *panopticon* which was designed not only as a prison but also as a factory. Yet the seemingly random character of play—mere dalliance—hardly squares with the current concern with play as a problem. Play is not only a $30-billion industry but, as David Riesman[10] along with several Congressional investigating committees have noted, is a part of the business relation itself. Martha Wolfenstein and Nathan Leites call attention to the emergence of a "fun morality": fun is not simply permissible, it is obligatory.[11] If persons do not have fun, they experience shame or feelings of inadequacy. An Israeli army officer, on his return from the U.S.A. where he had been sent to absorb the latest in techniques of physical training, described to the writer his bewilderment:

I know men need a reason—a motivation. Who will march in the desert if he does not have to? But the real reason has always been enough for our men: they were preparing for possible battle. Practice. In America I learned about "fun." I tell you, my friend, that was something new. I was told that physical training must be designed so that the men could enjoy it. Enjoy it, you hear? Even cleanup—kitchen-police, toilets—had to be made fun. "Make a game of it," I was advised.

Now look here. Anybody who is so stupid that he can be convinced that cleaning toilets is enjoyable would not pass the admission requirements into the Israeli army. You do these things because you must, with your mind on your ultimate purpose. Not for fun. Will a man lay down his life in battle for fun?

Although this officer was deploring what he felt was a mockery of serious activity by the invasion of play, his basic bewilderment was with the reverse phenomenon: play itself—the game—becomes a dead-serious activity dedicated to goals outside itself and therefore instrumental and no longer pursued for the sheer joy of it.

It is my belief that the foregoing two themes—work as instrumental *vs.* leisure and play as expressive, and work as compulsory *vs.* play as voluntary or free—do not carry us sufficiently far in theoretical analysis. Leisure and work are related but direct contrasts do not exhaust the range of possibilities. An alternative method of shedding light on the relation may be explored through the use of functional theory. The role of work as a functional imperative has been central to such theory; the equally important role of play has not been explored to my knowledge, except incidentally. My remarks will, therefore, focus on leisure and play. Since the latter *are* usually defined in terms of aimless dalliance, the proposal to examine their functions should prove instructive not only for the study of leisure but for functional theory itself.

It is maintained that play, far from being a frivolous activity, or, alternatively, a problem, only, that has gotten out of hand, is essential to the existence of a social system. An analogy worth thinking about is presented by the fact that engineers speak of the need for a minimum of "play" in the parts of a machine:

for example, belts that are too tight will snap under stress. One wonders immediately about play in this sense—slippage—in social systems. Meetings of professional societies are generally not precisely planned, perhaps inadvertently. Yet if a proposal for moment-to-moment planning of events were made, one would be justified in urging a certain looseness. Some members will gnash their teeth that sessions are slow in following one another, but such looseness allows for corridor-talk, job-hunting, and on-the-spot arrangements that persons who meet casually may wish to make.

Rather, however, than proceeding with the enumeration of such examples, we shall proceed systematically to examine the central role of play and leisure in the solution of the four major functional problems of social systems as those have been identified by R. F. Bales, Talcott Parsons, and Edward Shils;[12] namely, pattern maintenance and tension management, adaptation, goal attainment, and integration.

Pattern Maintenance and Tension Management

The crucial position of play in the process of societal socialization has been described so often that it needs little more than passing reference here.[13] G. H. Mead categorized a significant part of the process as that of taking the role of others through playing and playing at roles. Cooley felt "sympathy," in the technical sense, to underlie the sentiments, making up a universal human nature. It is noteworthy also that storytelling—among the most universal of all forms of play—is used everywhere as a teaching technique (the sugar-coated pill) from *Aesop's Fables* to *The Little Engine That Could*. Play is equally important in the socialization of adults into work organizations but since space forbids an extended discussion, we shall content ourselves with one note. Work learning includes technical skills, tricks of the trade, and social skills, the latter dealing with work norms, accepted social behavior, accepted attitudes, work codes, *etc*. It is precisely such social skills that are most difficult to teach apart from the job and yet are so crucial that special techniques are employed to be sure they are deeply internalized. One of the commonest of such techniques is that of horseplay:

the novice finds his tools missing, completed parts disappear, he is sent on errands to nonexistent places for nonexistent tools, his youth is the object of obscene jokes—such procedures serving both to teach and to impress on the newcomer the role of tyro.

Culture patterns must, of course, not only be learned but continually renewed and reaffirmed, a task usually accomplished by ritual and symbolic behavior. It seems to be universally the case that play, and often sport accompany ceremony in such forms as dancing, feasting and other modes of expressive behavior. Lasswell's definition of the super-ego as that part of the personality which is soluble in alcohol[14] is relevant, for alcohol not only accompanies much expressive play behavior but is itself a potent agent for freeing bodily resources for further expression, at least up to a point.

It is relevant also to point to the way in which cherished societal values are often incorporated into games. "Fair play" is sometimes found only in sports where it functions to keep the ideal, at least, pure, and when violated, may produce such a howl of public outrage as is rarely heard in any other sphere of social life. Many have noted that highly competitive sports, whatever their costs to those who fail are especially important in a culture emphasizing success goals, a phenomenon that has made sports a fertile breeding ground for heroes. And it is apt, also, because its heroes are likely to be young: there is nothing surprising about a champion athlete who is twenty-five years of age or less for if a man is ever going to be a champion, he will have to make it by then or he will not make it at all. This, in turn, means that there is often a rapid ascent from an obscure beginning—skyrocket mobility.[15] And since skill is so important in sports, and different social backgrounds are often submerged in the near nudity of the boxer or the uniform of the player, there may result such a close approach to purity of competition as to be dramatically irresistible. The "moment of truth" is celebrated in bull-fighting, not in meatpacking.

In the area of tension management, the cathartic and restorative functions of leisure are preeminent, from the parlor-room joke to the ritualized functions of spectatorship. Gregory Stone suggests that "the sports pages in the daily newspaper

are important for many consumers primarily because they
provide some confirmation that there is a continuity in the events
and affairs of the larger society."[16] He also calls attention to
the role of camping for men in reaffirming masculinity, or
perhaps in escaping it.[17] In work situations, a special function
of the colleague group—the group of mutually-trusting equals
who drink coffee or play cards together—is of central importance.
In medicine, no matter how experienced you are, some of your
patients are going to die; in criminal law, no matter how
eloquent you are, some of your clients are going to the electric
chair; in teaching, no matter how skilled you are, some of your
students are going to fail; in the priesthood, no matter how
hard you pray for them, some of the souls in your charge are
going straight to hell. The major function of colleague groups
is to prevent one from cracking up in the face of significant
failure. It is essential to one's self confidence that there be a
group with whom one can take a friendly glass, and these
persons must be more than mere friends. They must be colleagues whose reassurance counts and who can be counted upon
to understand.[18]

Adaptation

Leisure and play have functions in the adaptive sphere precisely where instrumental values have primacy. Work results,
inevitably, in fatigue and often in boredom, and one of the
forms of leisure—recreation—is essential here insofar as it restores,
though, it is recognized, it may not always do so. In a perceptive
discussion of the functions of voluntary associations, Arnold Rose
points to the fact that "the opportunity to engage in something
creative, even if only in a hobby association, provides a compensation for the deadening effect of working on a simple
repetitive task on the modern production line."[19] Play, though
it might conceivably do so, seems rarely to provide practice in
skills relevant to job proficiency, though one may try to convert
practice into play as the Israeli officer commented above. More
important seem to be the ubiquitous informal groups in industry,
groups distinguished by the fact their members spend so much
of their time in joking, smoking, loafing, hanging around the

water-cooler and other activities which, if not all play, are certainly not work. The literature in industrial sociology is replete with discussions of the functions of informal groups among which are communication between work departments, mutual support and help in time of work stress, enforcement of work norms and implementation of sanctions on deviant workers as well as other functions.[20] From management's point of view, such behavior may be dysfunctional; from the worker's, it may be adaptive.

Malinowski long ago wrote that though the Kula involves trade in armshells and necklaces, neither of these objects is worn much or even displayed conspicuously. However, incidental to the Kula, a good deal of trading in ordinary objects does go on. Similarly, the fact that a very large industry goes on to supply the means by which persons may have fun has been heavily documented.[21] And where persons come to have a business interest in recreation, we get advertising and other pressures to enjoy oneself so that the supplier of enjoyment may be able to enjoy himself as well. Finally, in the adaptive context, we draw attention to a phenomenon whose complexity forbids other than mere reference to it: we mean play as motivation. For most persons, work is motivated, without doubt, by the need and desire for necessaries and other things that money will buy. But such a statement, while true enough, is too global, for behavior must be motivated not only from pay-day to pay-day but from moment to moment. Habit will carry a worker so far, and the rewards of activity per se will carry one a little further, but then boredom or conflicting desires will intervene. Clement Greenberg has spoken of the fact that traditional work included customs, rites and observances which "furnished occasions *inside* work for relief from the strain of its purposefulness."[22] With the emphasis on efficiency, such incidental or accompanying activities were eliminated and work was made, by that means, more tense and demanding. The contrast between shopping for goods in the U. S. and shopping in much of the rest of the world, especially outside the English-speaking area, is instructive. While waiting for service in a queue in an Israeli shop, the writer expressed exasperation to another man at our having to wait while a woman shopper at the front of the line chatted informally with the shopkeeper about private matters. "Don't fret yourself," answered the man to me. "These women have a hard day at home. This is an outing. It's their only form of recreation." My companion was, I am sure, exaggerating. In view of Kinsey's finding that there is an average of only one pregnancy per 1,000 copulations in the U. S., Nelson Foote's reference to this "favorite form of play for millions of Americans"[23] probably applies, at least partially, to other countries too.

Goal Attainment

We have not drawn strict distinctions among the often overlapping categories of leisure, play, games, sport, recreation, hobbies and fun, but we recognize that Johan Huizinga[24] has assigned to play and Josef Pieper[25] (as well as many others) to leisure a primary role in culture. The leisure classes of past civilizations often assumed or arrogated to themselves a public responsibility which included the protection and celebration of the primary symbols and ultimate values of the culture, however much the leisure class might, in the process, profit by a monopoly over the means of access to those symbols.

Central in goal attainment as a functional problem is the problem of allocation of members to appropriate and needed positions. The use of differential reward includes assigning differential access to leisure and consumption opportunities, and these are often as distinctive as productive occupations, as R. Clyde White,[26] for example, has described. But the increasing availability of leisure objects through purchase forces upper classes to retire deeper into the steadfasts of exclusive clubs.

A special mechanism of allocation in work situations is the frequent use of informal means of sizing up new members of organizations, especially when social skills are important in the job. Elsewhere[27] the writer has described the deliberate use by an Air Force major of poker as a means of estimating his men's stamina under social pressure, reactions to losing and to winning, ability to concentrate while holding one's liquor, ability to keep one's head under stress, and so forth. Few employers go so far but certainly the coffee-break serves as an occasion for sizing one another up and developing mutual confidence (as well as the reverse).

Integration

Bales'[28] analysis of the phase-sequence in problem-solving in small groups calls attention to the need to restore solidarity since concentration on goal attainment produces frictions and tensions. A major means of doing so is through group sociability —interaction as an end in itself rather than for the sake of the group goal. G. C. Homans[29] points to the fact that much of the behavior in the "internal system" of the Bank Wiring Observation Room at Western Electric consisted of "horsing around" and had integrative functions.

A special feature is presented by the wide appeal of play and sports activities. Chess seems to cross national boundaries with ease and is one of the few activities we will agree to engage in with the Russians. Within a society, play assumes a function analogous to the incest taboo, as noted by Talcott Parsons[30] and by George P. Murdock,[31] in preventing in-breeding or over-insulation of groups and organizations from one another. Sports are significant as foci of group identification also, as many social analysts have pointed out. In turn, the hierarchically organized tournament serves to restore the inter-group cleavage that may result. It is Washington against California, but later the Pacific Coast against the Big Ten, then, occasionally, the U. S. against Russia.

The foregoing analysis, like much functional analysis, has focused on problems whose solution is necessary for the survival of social systems. Yet a theoretical problem remains, for if we restrict our attention to survival only, creatures other than man have done better and will probably outlast him: the cockroach and the rat seem better adapted to urban life than does man. What is, after all, distinctive of man, and most interesting is not merely that he survives, but the goals to which he dedicates himself. The means man adopts are ingenious: culture is a most remarkable adaptive mechanism. But it is man's ends that make him human. G. K. Chesterton concludes his critical survey of the novelist Dickens with this appraisal:

But this at least is part of what (Dickens) meant; that comradeship and serious joy are not interludes in our travel; but
that rather our travels are interludes in comradeship and joy. . . .
The inn does not point to the road; the road points to the inn.[32]

David Riesman[33] reverses an earlier position and in a recent
essay calls for the deliberate infusion of challenge and meaning
into work, for he feels that leisure has become as mechanized
and as compulsive as work, hence offering little hope for man's
development and growth. Arnold Rose, on the other hand, points
out that voluntary associations offer a powerful mechanism of
social change: "As soon as a felt need for some social change
arises, one or more voluntary associations immediately springs
up to try to secure the change."[34] Of course voluntary associations are only rarely exclusively recreational but sociability
and play are usually important secondary, if not primary activities in them. The clue here is that leisure and play provide a
fruitful ground for the examination of functional problems other
than those of survival, especially those involved not simply in
goal attainment but in goal-definition, particularly as the latter
relate to or require change and invention. For work, however,
joyful it is to a *kibbutznik*,[35] however absorbing to a researcher,
or however challenging it might be made, remains, for most
persons, a means. Play and leisure may be means also, but only
persons at leisure *can* concern themselves with ends.

NOTES

1. Jean Piaget, *Play, Dreams and Imitation in Childhood* (New
York: W. W. Norton, 1951), pp. 147-50.
2. Margaret Mead, "The Pattern of Leisure in Contemporary
American Culture," *Annals of the American Academy of Political and
Social Science*, 313 (September, 1957), pp. 11-15, esp. p. 13.
3. Don Martindale, *American Society* (Princeton, N. J.: D. Van
Nostrand, 1960), p. 432, and Chapter 18 *passim*.
4. Georg Simmel, *The Sociology of Georg Simmel* (trans. by
Kurt H. Wolff; Glencoe, Ill.: The Free Press, 1950), p. 42.
5. Gregory P. Stone, "American Sports: Play and Dis-Play,"

reprinted in Eric Larrabee and Rolf Meyersohn (eds.), *Mass Leisure* (Glencoe, Ill.: The Free Press, 1958), pp. 261-62.

6. Daniel Bell, *The End of Ideology* (Chicago, Ill.: The Free Press of Glencoe, 1960) p. 246.

7. The Editors of Fortune, "$30 Billion for Fun," reprinted in Eric Larrabee and Rolf Meyersohn (eds.) *Mass Leisure, op. cit.*, p.160.

8. Johan Huizinga, *Homo Ludens* (London: Routledge and Kegan Paul, 1949), p. 8.

9. Gregory P. Stone and Marvin J. Taves, "Camping in the Wilderness," reprinted in Eric Larrabee and Rolf Meyersohn (eds.), *Mass Leisure, op. cit.*, p. 296.

10. David Riesman *et al.*, *The Lonely Crowd* (New Haven: Yale University Press, 1950), Chapter VII.

11. Martha Wolfenstein and Nathan Leites, *Movies: A Phychological Study* (Glencoe, Ill.: The Free Press, 1950), p. 21.

12. See Talcott Parsons, Robert F. Bales and Edward A. Shils, *Working Papers in the Theory of Action* (Glencoe, Ill.: The Free Press, 1953), pp. 183-86; Talcott Parsons, "A Revised Analytical Approach to the Theory of Social Stratification," in Reinhard Bendix and Seymour M. Lipset (eds.), *Class, Status and Power: A Reader in Social Stratification* (Glencoe, Ill.: The Free Press, 1953), pp. 395-97, and 415-39; and Talcott Parsons and Neil J. Smelser, *Economy and Society* (Glencoe, Ill.: The Free Press, 1956), pp. 46-51.

13. Nor would documentation serve any useful purpose.

14. Referred to by Martha Wolfenstein in "The Emergence of Fun Morality," *Journal of Social Issues*, 7 (No. 4, 1951), p. 22.

15. The result, however, is more likely to be a hero than a success. See Edward Gross, *Work and Society* (New York: Thomas Y. Crowell Co., 1958), p. 193, n. 73. See also Orrin Klapp, "The Creation of Popular Heroes," *American Journal of Sociology*, 54 (September, 1948), pp. 135-41.

16. Gregory P. Stone, "American Sports: Play and Dis-Play," *op. cit.*, p. 256.

17. *Ibid.*, p. 259.

18. On the functions of colleagueship, see Edward Gross, *Work and Society, op. cit.*, pp. 235-41.

19. Arnold Rose, *Sociology* (New York: Knopf, 1956), p. 330.

20. See, for example, Edward Gross, *Work and Society, op. cit.*, pp. 251-55; and Eugene V. Schneider, *Industrial Sociology* (New York: McGraw-Hill, 1957), pp. 193-202.

21. See, for example, The Editors of Fortune, "$30 Billion for Fun," *op. cit.*, and George Soule, "The Economics of Leisure," *Annals of the American Academy of Political and Social Science*, 313 (Sept., 1957), pp. 16-24.

22. Clement Greenberg, "Work and Leisure Under Industrialism," *Commentary*, 16 (July, 1953), p. 58.

23. Nelson N. Foote, "Sex As Play," *Social Problems*, 1 (April, 1954), p. 161.

24. Johan Huizinga, *Homo Ludens, op. cit.*, esp. Chap. 12.

25. Josef Pieper, *Leisure, the Basis of Culture* (New York: Pantheon Books, 1952).

26. R. Clyde White, "Social Class Differences in the Uses of Leisure," *American Journal of Sociology*, 61 (September, 1955), pp. 145-50.

27. Edward Gross, "Some Functional Consequences of Primary Controls in Formal Work Organizations," *American Sociological Review*, 18 (Aug., 1953), pp. 368-73, esp. p. 372.

28. Robert F. Bales, "Adaptive and Integrative Changes As Sources of Strain in Social Systems," in A. Paul Hare, Edgar F. Borgatta, and Robert F. Bales (eds.), *Small Groups* (New York: Knopf, 1955), pp. 127-31.

29. George C. Homans, *The Human Group* (New York: Harcourt-Brace, 1950), pp. 150-55.

30. Talcott Parsons, "The Incest Taboo in Relation to Social Structure and the Socialization of the Child," *British Journal of Sociology*, 5 (June, 1954), pp. 101-17. See n. 12, p. 117.

31. George P. Murdock, *Social Structure* (New York: Macmillan, 1949), p. 296.

32. G. K. Chesterton, *Charles Dickens: A Critical Study* (New York: Dodd, Mead, 1911), p. 300.

33. David Riesman, "Leisure and Work in Post-Industrial Society," in Eric Larrabee and Rolf Meyersohn (eds.), *Mass Leisure, op. cit.*, pp. 363-85.

34. Arnold Rose, *Sociology, op. cit.*, p. 331.

35. Melford E. Spiro in *Kibbutz: Venture in Utopia* (Cambridge: Harvard University Press, 1956), wrote that, to a resident of a *kibbutz* (a *kibbutznik*), his job ". . . becomes more than a way of making a living. It becomes a *sacred task*, a calling, in the religious sense of that term . . ." p. 89.

ROBERT DUBIN

University of Oregon

3

Industrial Workers' Worlds: A Study of the "Central Life Interests" of Industrial Workers*

IN AN URBAN INDUSTRIAL SOCIETY it seems more than pertinent to inquire into the world of industrial workers. We are here concerned with defining this world in terms of the significant areas of social experience. For each area of experience our basic object is to determine whether it represents a life interest of importance to the worker. In particular, we will focus attention on work and the workplace to determine its standing as a central life interest to workers in industry.

The impact of industrialization and urbanization on human behavior is empirically noted and theoretically accounted for in the general sociological literature. Microscopic studies of industrial organizations and of "human relations" within them are producing their own observations and generalizations. The bodies of knowledge in general sociology and in industrial sociology are at variance on critical points. This study presents one part of a larger research linking general and industrial sociology. The linkage is made through an intensive study of the "central life interests" of industrial workers.

---
* Reprinted from *Social Problems*, Vol. 3, No. 3, January, 1956, this article was one of two presented with the Helen L. DeRoy Award in 1955.

Introduction

It is a commonplace to note that work has long been considered a central life interest for adults in most societies, and certainly in the Western world. Indeed, the capitalist system itself is asserted to rest upon the moral and religious justification that the Reformation gave to work, as Weber[1] and Tawney[2] have pointed out. Our research shows that for almost three out of every four industrial workers studied, work and the workplace *are not* central life interests.

This result is surely not startling to the general sociologist. He has already noted that the social world of urban man is continuously subdivided into areas of activity and interest, with each social segment lived out more or less independently of the rest. It seems highly plausible that the urban world, with its emphasis upon secondary and instrumental social relations, might indeed be one in which work has become secondary as a life interest.

The one large subject matter illuminated by industrial sociologists in the past decade has been the human relationships that surround job and task performance in the formal organizations of modern life.[3, 4, 5] We are generally led to believe that informal human relationships at work are important to the individual industrial man—he finds that the informal work society presents opportunities for intimate and primary human interaction. Our research indicates that only about 10 per cent of the industrial workers perceived their important primary social relationships as taking place at work. The other 90 per cent preferred primary interactions with fellowmen elsewhere than on the job!

This finding should jolt the industrial sociologist, if duplicated in subsequent studies. The result will be an important corrective to the naive assumption that complex and rational organizations of modern society, through which most of the society's business gets done, are effective or not as the human relations of their members are "good" or "bad."

In an era when loyalty is in the vocabulary of even the common man, the ways in which members become attached to and thereby loyal toward an organization are of central interest. Our research findings indicate that more than three out of five industrial workers have strong job-oriented preferences for those sectors of their experience that involve either a formal organization or technological aspects of their personal environment. This result (again perhaps surprising to the human relations expert) suggests that strong bonds of organization may be forged out of the impersonal aspects of work experience that attach the individual more or less firmly to his company or workplace.

These three problems taken together, then, are the subject of this report: (*a*) work as a central life interest; (*b*) the role and importance of primary social relations on the job; and (*c*) some sources of organizational attachment.

Theory

The theory underlying this study involves five basic points: (*a*) the axiom that social experience is inevitably segmented; (*b*) the assumption that an individual's social participation may be necessary in one or more sectors of his social experience but may not be important to him; (*c*) the logical conclusion that adequate social behavior will occur in sectors of social experience which are mandatory for social participation by the individual but not important to him; (*d*) the second conclusion that in situations of necessary but unimportant social participation the most direct and obvious features of the situation become bases for the individual's attachment to that situation; and (*e*) the third conclusion that primary social relations take place only in situations where the social experience is valued by the individual.

The axiom with which we start scarcely needs elaboration. The segmented character of experience is revealed in the round of daily activities where one kind of activity succeeds another; in the succession of days, and particularly the weekend days when leisure-time activity replaces remunerative work; in the physical separation of such significant locales as place of residence and place of work; and in the numerous autonomous organizations that serve special, and sometimes very esoteric,

interests in our lives. This by no means exhausts the illustrations
of ways in which social experience is divided into discrete parts,
but it should serve adequately to demonstrate the reasonableness
of our initial axiom.

It is equally obvious that participation in some segments or
sectors of social experience may be necessary but not important
to an individual. The significance of this assumption rests on
the definition of important social experience. We are here concerned with a subjective state of mind. Some social experience
is important because it is valued by its participants; some is
important because it is necessary as a means towards an end,
though slightly valued in itself. The ceremonial banquet for
awarding football letters to the college team may be valued as
public recognition of achievement. The meal eaten at the banquet
is important, too, but only as the justification for naming the
ceremony, not for its nutritive value or esthetic appeal. The kind
of importance we are concerned with is illustrated by the ceremony, not the meal.

This assumption tells us that social experience is differentially
valued. The form in which it is stated emphasizes the fact that
participation takes place in some experiences because it is necessary and not because the activity is itself valued. We could
equally well state the axiom as follows: only a portion of all
social experience is important or valued by its participants. We
have chosen the first formulation because it gives greater emphasis to the subject matter of this research—the fact that
remunerative work may be required by the society but that this
does not guarantee that it will be viewed as important or
valued by workers.

Three propositions or generalized predictions follow from our
two axioms. The first is that individuals will exhibit adequate
social behavior in sectors of social experience in which participation is mandatory but not valued. This proposition, when
converted to hypothesis form, becomes empirically testable. In
its proposition form it makes a general prediction for any and all
individuals. In the form of a hypothesis the prediction is limited
to the particular data of the study and the actual empirical
indicators used. For example, this proposition in our study be-

comes the following hypothesis: a significant proportion of industrial workers will rate non-job interests high in their value orientation on the Central Life Interests questionnaire. Our hypothesis as a prediction is completely consonant with the general proposition, but it is also directly related to the data of our study. The hypothesis is the bridge between the general proposition and the empirical data marshaled in testing the proposition. Any proposition can be converted to an indefinite number of hypotheses. Consequently, no confirmation of a single hypothesis can establish any proposition. The confirmed hypothesis does, however, lend support to the proposition. Our research findings lend support to the three propositions set forth. We are not, of course, asserting that the propositions are thereby proven.

The second proposition or general prediction is that an individual's attachment to a situation in which his social experience is not valued by him will be to the most physically and directly obvious characteristics of that situation. The pertinent hypotheses that flow from this proposition will be set forth below.

The third general prediction in proposition form is that primary human relations take place only in situations where the social experience is valued by the individual. By "primary human relations" we mean, of course, the relationships that occur in groups where the interaction is face-to-face, continuous, intimate, and shared over a wide range of subjects. The directly related hypotheses will be stated below.

Research Procedure

This study was conducted in 1952-53 in three Midwestern plants employing a total of approximately 1,200 workers. The companies are located in different communities ranging in size from 35,000 to 125,000, all clearly urban units. The largest company makes industrial equipment, employing about 600 workers on two shifts in a wide and typical range of metal manufacturing and equipment assembly operations. The smallest company manufactures industrial, dress, and novelty gloves of cloth and leather with a work force of approximately 200 employees, who were represented by an A.F. of L. union. The third company produces printed and novelty advertising items and employs about 400 people.

Active cooperation was secured in each plant to carry on the total study, which included observation of work performance and work behavior, the anonymous completion of a series of separate questionnaires administered over a period of time and completed by 491 workers, and intensive recorded interviews with a sample of 120 selected employees.

We will report here the results of the Central Life Interests questionnaire only. This questionnaire was designed to determine whether the job and workplace were central life interests of workers or whether other areas of their social experience were important to them. We defined "central life interest" as the expressed preference for a given locale or situation in carrying out an activity. After a pretest, forty questions were selected for the Central Life Interests (CLI) schedule.

Each question represented an activity that had an approximately equal likelihood of occurring in connection with some aspect of the job or workplace, or at some definite point in the community outside of work. A third choice was added that represented an indifferent or neutral response to the question. An example of a typical question is the following:

I would most hate
.... missing a day's work
.... missing a meeting of an organization I belong to
.... missing almost anything I usually do

The forty questions used dealt with the formal aspects of membership and behavior in organizations, the technological aspects of the environment, the informal group life experiences, and general everyday experiences. Each question was individually scored as a job-oriented response, as a non-job-oriented response, or as an indifferent response. The questions that applied to each of the four areas were then scored as separate groups by summing the responses to the individual questions in each group. Those workers who chose a work-related response on at least half the questions in each group and answered the remaining ones with a non-job or indifferent response, or who had at least 70 per cent of their answers made up of a combination of job-oriented and indifferent responses, were designated job-oriented workers. The remaining workers were designated non-job in their outlook because they responded with more emphasis upon non-job and indifferent choices. The indifferent response is not utilized as a separate category in this report.

By the same scoring procedure and using the same criteria a total classification was secured for each worker. This indicated whether he was job-oriented or non-job-oriented in his total pattern of responses on all forty questions.

Work As a Central Life Interest

Previous researchers have generally assumed that work must be a central life interest because so many are engaged in it. We make quite a different assumption about work. We assume that holding a job is simply evidence of adequate performance above some minimal level that justifies continued employment by the company. In short, we assume that social behavior is adequate in this sector of social experience. For us the research question becomes one of determining to what extent the job and its locale are central life interests to workers.

It will be recalled that our first proposition is that individuals will exhibit adequate social behavior in sectors of social experience in which participation is mandatory but not valued. Remunerative work is mandatory both in the general sense that most male adults (or female heads of households) are expected to work for a living and in the specific sense that each job is surrounded by many imperatives and requirements for its performance. We have thus assumed that continued employment is evidence of adequacy of social behavior and that holding a paying job is evidence of mandatory participation in the two senses mentioned.

Our hypothesis can now be stated as follows: a significant proportion of industrial workers will be classified as non-job-oriented when central life interest is measured with the CLI questionnaire.

Considering the pattern of responses to all the questions, we found that only 24 per cent of all the workers* studied could be labelled job-oriented in their life interests. Thus, three out of four of this group of industrial workers did not see their jobs and work places as central life interests for themselves. They found their preferred human associations and preferred areas of behavior outside of employment.

If this finding holds generally, the role and significance of work in American society has departed from its presumed historical position. Factory work may now very well be viewed by industrial workers as a means to an end—a way of acquiring income for life in the community. The factory as a locale for living out a lifetime seems clearly secondary to other areas of central life interest. The factory and factory work as sources of personal satisfaction, pride, satisfying human associations, perhaps even of pleasure in expressing what Veblen called the "instinct of workmanship," seem clearly subordinated in the American scene. The general and specific implications of this finding will be examined in the last section of this report.

Work and Informal Social Relations

Our third general prediction of human behavior in proposition form was that primary human relations take place only in situations where social experience is valued by the individual. From the test of our first hypothesis we have strong evidence that the workplace does not provide social experience that is valued more highly than other experiences. It would follow, then, that we may expect a significant proportion of industrial workers to be non-job-oriented with respect specifically to informal group experiences when measured on the relevant portion of the CLI questionnaire. This is the hypothesis derived from the above proposition.

Informal group experiences are those relations between people that are not directly a product of an official relationship in an organization or related positions in a division of labor. Illustrative of informal social relations are those involving small talk,

---

* N = 491, for this and all other percentages reported here.

leisure-time behavior, friendship interactions, and affectional attachments. Questions such as the following were asked:

> I would rather take my vacation
> .... with my family
> .... with some friends from work
> .... by myself
>
> The people I would be most likely to borrow money from are
> .... the people I know around town
> .... anyone who would lend it to me
> .... the people I know here in the plant
>
> It hurts me more if I am disliked
> .... by the people at work
> .... by the people around town
> .... by anyone I know

In all a total of fourteen questions were used to sample informal group experiences. A job-oriented or non-job-oriented score was secured for each worker for the informal group experience sector in accordance with the procedure set forth above.

Only 9 per cent of the industrial workers in the sample prefer the informal group life that is centered in the job. Nine out of ten of those studied clearly indicated that their preferred informal human associations and contacts were found in the community, among friends, and in the family.

The industrial sociologist has been impressive in demonstrating the informal group life of people associated together at work. But the relative significance of this kind of human experience in relation to the full round of life has never before been considered. If our findings are at all typical—and general sociology theory would predict the findings to be of this sort— then the workplace is not very congenial to the development of preferred informal human relationships.

Much action research and some company policy has implicitly or explicitly been grounded in the simple-minded assumption that improving, enriching, or facilitating the development of informal group life is both desirable as a goal (to develop "happy" workers) and necessary as a means (to improve production, decrease turnover, etc.). Now it can perhaps be suggested that, on balance, such well-intended efforts may be misdirected. The workplace is not the breeding ground of preferred informal human relationships; deliberate efforts to make it so may be relatively ineffectual. The possible exception, perhaps, is the one worker in ten who sees the job environment as his most likely source of desired informal group life.

The immediately preceding hypothesis tested its underlying proposition by asking questions directly about primary or informal social relations. We can make another test of the proposition by focusing upon the part of it that deals with valued social experience. One of the direct ways of getting at valued social experience is to ask questions that deal with activities giving pleasure, satisfaction, or general rewards, which may be pursued in varying places and at varying times. For questions dealing with this area we have used the designation of "general experience." In terms of this approach to our third proposition, the hypothesis becomes: a significant proportion of industrial workers will not respond to work as a valued social experience when this is tested by the general experience section of the CLI questionnaire. Questions dealing with general experience include those concerning "the most important things I do," "the most pleasant things I do," "my ideas about getting ahead," "my worries," and "my interests." General experience was sampled in a total of nine questions on the basis of which each worker was classified as job-oriented or non-job-oriented in this area.

Only 15 per cent of the workers give job-oriented preferences. The rest—about eleven in thirteen—saw experiences of theirs that were sampled in the study as taking place somewhere away from the workplace.

It is immediately suggested that the emotional impact of work and the work environment seems to be remarkably low in terms of general life experiences. Not only is the workplace relatively unimportant as a place of preferred primary human relationships, but it cannot even evoke significant sentiments and emotions in its occupants. These two conclusions may, of course, be related. A large proportion of emotionally significant experience takes place in primary group relationships. If the informal work group is a matter of relative indifference to workers, then it is reasonable that general social experiences of emotional importance will not take place with high frequency in the workplace.

It seems fair to conclude that our hypotheses have been supported. When measured in terms of valued social experience, the workplace is preferred by only 15 per cent of the workers studied. When measured in terms of primary human relations, only 9 per cent of the workers report that the workplace provides their preferred associations. Thus, in terms of the workplace as a testing ground, we can conclude that the underlying proposition may well be valid: primary human relations take place only in situations where social experience is valued by the individual. Obviously, many more tests of this proposition must be made, but the present tests encourage its future exploration.

Some Bases of Organizational Attachment

Max Weber has pointed out that, in formal organizations based upon rational authority with staff units organized in bureaucracies, the staff members are loyal to the legally established impersonal order of the organization.[6] By implicit extension of this idea we can see immediately the possibilities of other sources of organizational attachment for members. In particular, we can examine the possibility that organizational attachment can be a product of the formal organization and its operations, and of the technology which surrounds work.

Our second general proposition was set forth in the following manner: an individual's attachment to a situation in which his social experience is not valued by him will be to the most physically and directly obvious characteristics of that situation. From our data we propose to test this in terms of experience in formal organizations and experience with technology.

The choice of these two kinds of experiences is based on clear grounds. Both kinds of experiences are direct and obvious. We have many daily evidences of our participation in an organization. We arrive at its building from home, enter into a specified location, do required jobs under the direction of organization supervisors, work with machines and equipment under operating conditions that are special to the work, and have our time spent and output measured and recorded as a basis for remuneration.

We know from the first portion of this study that a significantly large percentage of the industrial workers studied do not value the work situation in terms of its opportunities for informal group experiences and for general affective experiences. This suggests that the workplace provides an excellent opportunity to test our second proposition, because it generally meets the condition that it does not provide valued social experience for a large proportion of its participants. We can derive the following hypothesis from that proposition: a significant proportion of industrial workers will score job-oriented for their organizational experience when measured on the organizational section of the CLI schedule.

A sampling was made of typical relationships between members and organizations. Experience in the formal sector includes a number of different relationships between an organization, its officials, and its members. Hiring, joining, firing, disciplining, rewarding, directing, and ordering are illustrative of relationships of this sort. Some of these relationships were covered in the study and on the basis of his responses to seven questions, each worker was rated as job-oriented or non-job-oriented in the formal sector.

More than three out of five of the workers were scored as job-oriented with respect to their experiences in organizations: 61 per cent chose their companies as the most meaningful context to them when their life experiences in organizations were brought into their focus. Put another way, the most significant formal organization when judged in terms of standard and typical organizational ties and bonds is the employing one, the industrial company.

This conclusion should not be confused with the notion that these workers are saying they necessarily like their employer or the company for which they work. No such questions were included. The questions asked placed emphasis only upon choosing that situation or organizational context in which a particular behavior was best carried out, or in which the worker would most like to have it happen. Thus, he was asked to choose between getting a job promotion or "becoming a more important member in my club, church, or lodge"; between workplace or "an organization I belong to" as the locale where praise received produces greater happiness; between regretting most "missing a day's work" or "missing a meeting of an organization I belong to." These choices serve to illustrate the questions asked in order to seek information on attachment to the formal organizations in workers' lives. Like all the questions asked, those in the formal sector were designed to determine the central life interests of workers.

We may conclude, then, that the workers studied were not confusing a liking for their company or its officials with a preference for their workplace as the most important formal organization in their lives. It seems reasonably clear that a significant majority of these workers believed that the companies in which they worked provided the important or preferred opportunities for organizational experience. Further important implications of this finding will be examined below.

The second test of the general proposition underlying this section can be made through the following hypothesis: a significant proposition of industrial workers will be job-oriented for their experiences with technological aspects of their environments when measured on the technological section of the CLI questionnaire.

A sampling was made of experiences involving the relations between people and the technical aspects of their environment. The questions probing this aspect of experience gave the workers the opportunity to select the place or situation most preferred or desired for behavior directly involving relations with machines or technical operating conditions. The technical sector of experience was defined as that involving the relationships between an individual and his actual work operations. Tool, equipment, and machine maintenance; concern with job and operating techniques; overcoming operating problems; minimizing waste; accuracy of operations; quality of materials; and cleanliness and care of operations are illustrative of the kinds of relationships between an individual and technical aspects of his environment. These relations were sampled and another score on job vs.

non-job orientation was secured for each worker for the technological sector of experience, based on a total of ten questions.

In the technological sector, 63 per cent of the respondents were scored as job-oriented. This is the highest proportion of job-oriented responses for any of the sectors of experience examined. It certainly seems notable that almost two out of every three of the workers studied identified their workplace as the locale of their preferred relationships with the purely technical aspects of their environment.

The meaning of this finding can, perhaps, be made clearer when we examine some of the kinds of questions asked. For the statement, "I don't mind getting dirty," the alternative responses were: "while working at home," "at anytime if I can wash up afterwards," "while working at the plant." The introductory phrase, "I most enjoy keeping," was followed by these choices of response: "my things around the house in good shape," "my hand tools and workspace on the job in good shape," "my mind off such things." Additional questions in this area included:

Noise bothers me most
.... when working at home
.... when working at the plant
.... hardly ever

When I am doing some work
.... I am usually most accurate working at home
.... I seldom think about being accurate
.... I am usually most accurate working at the plant

It will be noted that an attempt was made to select those kinds of technical considerations that would have an equal likelihood of being relevant to the non-job and job environments. We feel certain that the high percentage of job-oriented responses is not the product of a bias in the questions asked that tended to favor the job environment.

The fact that the technological sector of experience is the most clearly job-oriented one suggests the desirability of a fresh appraisal of this dimension of social experience. In the past there has been considerable concern with the general meaninglessness of industrial work derived directly from a technology that makes work itself monotonous, repetitious, mechanical, and fragmentary. The human consequence of this has been generally assumed to be indifference, alienation, rebellion, or even personal disorganization and possibly mental disorder.

We can, however, return to one of Durkheim's important theoretical points and see another possible analytical approach to the problem of technology.[7] It will be recalled that Durkheim stressed the organic solidarity that made whole the individual units, tasks, and jobs in a given division of labor. He was emphasizing, of course, the necessary unity and integration that must bind together the divided and separate tasks and functions constituting the given division of labor. Without such unity the parts cannot mesh properly with each other with the result that the planned-for outcome (product or service) will not be forthcoming.

To Durkheim, this organic solidarity was a non-consensual one. People who were part of a given division of labor did not necessarily share with other members of it either a sense of common enterprise or a body of common values. To be sure, Durkheim clearly saw that consensus was essential to social unity, as his concept of mechanical solidarity illustrates. The connections between the two forms of social bond were a central research interest of his, but remain even to this day a set of mooted issues.

It may now be possible to suggest that industrial employment is one of the important focal points in our society for experiences with technical environments. This kind of experience has meaning in a sociological sense because it signifies the interdependence of man with man even where there is no necessary common ground of values shared between them. The urban environment is heterogeneous—in values, in the backgrounds of its residents, and in their daily experiences. Diversity is one of the hallmarks of urban life. But underpinning this heterogeneity and diversity is a fundamental human interdependence that flows from the far-flung division of labor. The real experiencing of this interdependence and sensing of it comes from the daily job. On the job the urbanite learns more directly and acutely than anywhere else how dependent he is upon those about him. There may follow from this the unity of interdependent action that is such an impressive feature of industrial work. This can often be achieved even in spite of lack of consensus, as Goode and Fowler neatly demonstrated in their study of an industrial plant.[8]

The characteristics of industrial work that are alleged to be disturbing to the individual (monotony, repetitiveness, mechanistic character, and over-specialization) are the very features that make obvious to its participants the nature of symbiotic or technological interdependence. In short, industrial work may be functional for the society because it sharply etches for the individual some awareness of the division of labor and its resultant interdependence.

Both of the hypotheses derived from our second proposition have been supported. This suggests that the proposition has merit. It certainly must be subjected to further test, but we now have some prospect that the tests will continue to sustain the general prediction about human behavior that it represents.

Conclusions

The industrial workers' world is one in which work and the workplace are not central life interests for a vast majority. In particular, work is not a central life interest for industrial workers when we study the informal group experiences and the general social experiences that have some affective value for them. Industrial man seems to perceive his life history as having its center outside of work for his intimate human relationships and for his feelings of enjoyment, happiness, and worth. On the other hand, for his experiences with the technological aspects of his life space and for his participation in formal organizations, he clearly recognizes the primacy of the workplace. In short, he has a well-developed sense of attachment to his work and workplace without a corresponding sense of total commitment to it.

In a more general sense this study has been designed to provide empirical tests for three propositions. We have evidence to believe that these propositions are worthy of further testing. It now seems reasonable to believe that individuals will exhibit adequate social behavior in sectors of social experience in which participation is mandatory but not valued. Where the social experience is not valued, the individual may still become attached to the situation of the experience in terms of the most physically and directly obvious features of that situation (as we examined it, the formal organization and its technology). Finally, we would predict that primary human relationships develop only in situations where the social experience is valued by the individual.

Implications and Speculations

Several years ago the Corning Glass Company celebrated its centennial with a conference whose proceedings have been published under the title of *Creating an Industrial Civilization.*[9] This suggests a theme for drawing implications from this study 'in a speculative vein. The emphasis is upon the future and the creative task that lies ahead.

Viewed from the standpoint of industrial management there are two broad and contradictory influences at work in the society. Work is no longer a central life interest for workers. These life interests have moved out into the community. Yet work was presumably once a central life interest. Much management activity in personnel and industrial relations is implicitly directed at restoring work to the status of a central life interest. Management's efforts and the main drift of social developments work at directly contrary purposes.

The second contradictory influence centers on the location of primary human relationships in the total social fabric. Some groups in management have accepted a philosophy and developed social engineering practices summed up in the phrase "human relations in industry." The major purpose of this movement is to center primary human relationships in work and make it functional for productivity. At the same time it seems evident that primary human relations are much more likely to be located at some place out in the community. The management efforts again seem to be at odds with social reality.

The first dilemma is perhaps best highlighted in the pronounced frustration that management practitioners experience with the relative failure of their efforts to engender a sense of participation in their work forces. Many have become convinced that it's all a matter of communication and semantics. If simple language is chosen, comic-book presentation is used, and volume of impact is raised, then employees will feel they are part of the "company team," a phrase commonly used. Other efforts have been directed at "participant management" and its latter-day descendant, "group dynamics." Here the chief goal seems to be to make a central life interest out of work by permitting some sharing by employees of decisions affecting their work routines.

None of these efforts has been crowned by remarkable success. Indeed, the group dynamics technique, which has much research background and a number of practical applications, seems singularly sterile. When the research findings indicate that the technique has not produced a material change in the output of an experimental group over an "old-fashioned" control group, the group dynamics approach is justified on the ground that it is easier on the emotional hide of those who are subjected to it.

Perhaps the issue is really not one of human manipulation after all. All the communication effort and group dynamics in the world will not alter the basic drift in our society away from a central life interest in work. Some of the older personnel techniques of supporting after-work activities, bowling leagues and bird-watching clubs, may really be more sensible. Company involvement in a constructive way in community affairs, in the non-work activities of its own employees as well as in a general sense, might be a more significant way to enhance attachment of employees to their company. Perhaps the basic problem is not one of central life interest in work after all, but one of enhancing the sense of attachment of participants to social organizations in which participation is necessary but not important to them. These are all questions that are suggestively derived from this study. They may be examined with profit.

The second dilemma has an interesting intellectual history in which theorizers and researchers, having established the concept of primary group and primary social relations, [10, 11] proceeded to apply it indiscriminately to all kinds of social organizations. Whyte in his finest study[12] gave us a magnificent picture of primary relations in boys' gangs (community, not work, organizations). He has since attempted to discover the same primary group life in industry,[13] with much less certainty of the results obtained. At least in this writer's opinion we have a good deal of evidence that there are non-official as well as official, or informal along with formal, relations in a business organization. But to call these "primary social relationships" may do grave injustice to a perfectly good concept.

It may very well be that those efforts of any managerial group in any kind of organization to center primary group life for a majority of employees in the workplace are misplaced. If our evidence is substantiated in other studies, the community is the locale of preferred primary social relations. To attempt to shift the locale to the workplace may be trying to reverse a social development that is not alterable in that direction.

This may not be an entirely undesirable prospect. Weber emphasized the impersonality and efficiency of modern bureaucratic organization. The efficiency can remain along with the impersonality, providing there are other points in the society where the primary social relations can be experienced.

The general conclusion of the Corning Glass Conference was that the problem of creating an industrial civilization is essentially a problem of social invention and creativity in the non-work aspects of life. Our great social inventions will probably not come in connection with work life; they will center in community life. This research certainly suggests the importance of this insight.

NOTES

1. Max Weber, *The Protestant Ethic and the Spirit of Capitalism* (London: Geo. Allen and Unwin, Ltd., 1930).

2. R. H. Tawney, *Religion and the Rise of Capitalism* (New York: Harcourt, 1926).

3. George C. Homans, *The Human Group* (New York: Harcourt, Brace and Co., 1950).

4. F. J. Roethlisberger and W. J. Dickson, *Management and the Worker* (Cambridge: Harvard University Press, 1934).

5. W. F. Whyte, *Human Relations in the Restaurant Industry* (New York: McGraw-Hill Book Co., 1948).

6. Max Weber, *Theory of Social and Economic Organization* (New York: Oxford University Press, 1947).

7. Emile Durkheim, *Division of Labor in Society* (Glencoe, Ill.: Free Press, 1947).

8. W. J. Goode and I. Fowler, "Incentive Factors in a Low Morale Plant," *American Sociological Review*, 14 (October, 1949), pp. 619-24.

9. *Creating an Industrial Civilization*, Eugene A. Staley, ed. (New York: Harper Bros., 1952).

10. C. H. Cooley, *Social Organization* (New York: Scribner, 1924).

11. Georg Simmel, *The Sociology of Georg Simmel*, K. H. Wolff ed. (Glencoe, Ill.: Free Press, 1950).

12. W. F. Whyte, *Street Corner Society* (Chicago: University of Chicago Press, 1943).

13. Whyte, *Human Relations in the Restaurant Industry, op. cit.*

LOUIS H. ORZACK

Boston University

4

Work as a "Central Life Interest" of Professionals*

ROBERT DUBIN'S study of the "central life interests" of industrial workers concluded that work and the workplace do not
generally constitute important foci of concern for this group.[1]
As Dubin suggests his study calls for replication with equivalent groups. It would seem desirable in addition to replicate
with other components of the labor force. Our knowledge of the
professions and of the pattern of commitment by professionals to
work-centered goals is extensive.[2] This knowledge leads to the
prediction that professionals would stress work and workplace
as preferred locations for a variety of activities. Hence, work is
more likely to be a "central life interest" for professionals than
it is for industrial workers. This paper reports the results of
an attempt to verify this prediction.

❁   ❁   ❁

Professionals' Patterns

It can hardly be assumed that professionals do not value
their work. They may in fact consider it an end in itself. For
the professional, work is a focal center of self-identification and
is both important and valued. Thus, we predict that profes-

---

* Reprinted from *Social Problems*, Vol. 7, No. 2, Fall, 1959. This is part
of a larger program of current research which analyzes and compares
the role orientations of members of different professions. It is carried on
with the support of the University of Wisconsin Graduate Research
Committee and with a grant from the Wisconsin Department of Nurses.

sionals will be much more favorably oriented to work as a "central life interest" than are industrial workers.

Training as a professional may stress technological details as well as the learning of behaviors appropriate to future roles in work settings. Such training also encourages aspirants to professional status to prefer a work setting to other settings for the location of informal social relationships and as sources of personal satisfactions; these, however, are not as readily codified for transmission during training as are technology and prescriptions involving organization roles. At most, preferences for work rather than non-work settings for the environment for informal social relationships and for general personal satisfactions may be considered to be probable, if unintended, consequences of necessary segregation during training. Preferences of this sort are not the planned outcome of specific curricular features.

From these considerations, we expect the pattern among the four components of experiences which Dubin reported for industrial workers to be duplicated with professionals. Professionals will be quite likely to prefer the environment of the workplace as the setting for technological and organizational experiences. They will to a lesser degree locate informal social relationships and general personal satisfactions within the arena of work. In all four sectors, however, professionals should weight work settings more heavily than they weight non-work settings.

Sources and Methods

Questionnaires which contained Dubin's "central life interest" items were administered to registered professional nurses employed in public and private general hospitals and a state mental hospital in a Midwestern city.[3] The cooperation of these institutions and of the registry organization of nurses employed on private duty in them was obtained. In all, 150 professional nurses completed questionnaires.

Scoring procedures were identical with those reported by Dubin, both for the calculation of the total pattern and for the sub-patterns. Results deriving from professional nurses, as well as those from Dubin's sample of industrial workers, are presented in Table 1.

TABLE 1

Total *"Central Life Interests"* and *Subordinate Experience Patterns,*
for Professional Nurses (*Orzack*) *and Industrial Workers* (*Dubin*)

Pattern	Professional Nurses (Orzack) Per Cent	Industrial Workers (Dubin) Per Cent
Total "Central Life Interest"		
Work	79	24
Non-work	21	76
Informal Relations		
Work	45	9
Non-work	55	91
General Relations (Personal Satisfactions)		
Work	67	15
Non-work	33	85
Formal Organization Relations		
Work	91	61
Non-work	9	39
Technological Relations		
Work	87	63
Non-work	13	37
N	150	491

Results

The most provocative finding concerns the total pattern.
Dubin reported that ". . . for almost three out of every four
industrial workers studied, work and the workplace *are not*
central life interests." In contrast, for four of every five nurses
studied, work and the workplace *are* central life interests. We
may infer that these professional nurses are much more interested in their work than Dubin's factory workers were in theirs.

The responses for the four sub-categories of experiences support in the main the relevant hypotheses. Informal social relations as well as general sources of personal satisfactions are less
likely to be work or job-centered than are experiences involving participation in formal organization and technological
behaviors. Professional nurses weight work settings more heavily

than they weight non-work settings, with one exception: informal relations are somewhat more closely linked with non-work and community locations than is the case for general personal satisfactions. Nurses are overwhelmingly likely to prefer work to non-work or community settings for their technological behavior and for their participation in formal organizations.

The responses of these professional nurses regarding the preferred centers of informal social relations and the preferred sources of personal satisfactions are interesting. Some 45 per cent of the respondents express a preference for work as the environment for informal social relations, with the remainder choosing non-work. About two thirds select work as the preferred source of personal satisfactions, with one-third reporting that non-work sources are preferred for these satisfactions.

The relations between these are complicated and deserve further scrutiny. It might be expected that informal social relationships, probably primary group memberships, would furnish the individual with lasting personal satisfactions. However, many of these respondents locate their sources of personal satisfactions in environments others than those which they prefer for informal social relationships. In Table 2, the respondents' choices of work and non-work locations for the two items under consideration are cross-tabulated. Almost 60 per cent select the same locations for both; of this group, virtually two-

TABLE 2

Work and Non-Work Choices for Informal Group Experiences and General Sources of Personal Satisfactions, by Professional Nurses

Informal Group	Sources of Personal Satisfactions		
Experiences	Work	Non-work	N
Work	53	14	67
	(35%)	(9%)	
Non-work	48	35	83
	(32%)	(23%)	
N	101	49	150
			(100%)

fifths indicate that their greatest personal satisfactions and most preferred informal group experiences come to them outside the environment of work. Clearly, these are professionals whose outlook on their work can be expected to be somewhat distinctive. This outlook might stress what Habenstein and Christ have called the "utilizer" orientation toward a professional role.[4] Neither the pro-science and technique-committed "professionalizer" nor the warm-hearted "traditionalizer" could readily be expected to have such a perspective. These responses might be typical of professionals who are engrossed in the area of work in any fundamental sense.

Somewhat similar problems arise in connection with the two other groups of nurses. One-third of all nurse respondents indicate they prefer work as the setting from which they derive personal satisfactions, while preferring non-work locations for their informal group participation. Nine per cent of the nurses make the opposite choices, they prefer work for informal group experiences, and non-work for their personal satisfactions. Thus, among these nurses with "deviant" orientations, the number who prefer work-centered personal satisfactions but non-work centered informal group experiences is roughly three and one-half times as great as those who prefer the alternate locations for their satisfactions and group experiences.

Training as a professional may be expected to instill rather deeply-felt motivations toward personal satisfactions in work activities. However, the sense of colleagueship might not be as fully developed or intensified in nursing as in other professions. For many, nursing is simply back-stop protection against the hazards of widowhood, ageing or spinsterhood. These professionals might be expected to have extensive memberships in what they would define as non-work groups, including their families and neighborhood associations. For many with tenuous commitments to nursing, the appeal of those memberships could far outweigh the significance of colleagues.

These non-professional memberships may levy diffuse demands upon the individuals involved; the appropriate role behavior for them is learned gradually and usually unwittingly. In contrast, colleague groups demand patterned and specified behaviors; the associated roles are achieved through specialized instruction during a limited time span. The kinds of overlapping commitments to non-work groups and to colleague groups for this profession, at least, can be clarified by the results given above. Specialized training produces an individual with particular technological skills who has been taught to find the work rewarding and satisfying. At the same time, the profession does not have appeals sufficient to outweigh role obligations required by non-professional groups in which its members participate.

Such a pattern may be especially characteristic of professions with many females. The critical feature is the transiency of the professionals and the limited commitment that ties the person with the specialty. Or, the pattern might be characteristic of work specialties which have not achieved full status as professions. This implies that the ability of an aspirant profession to dominate the behavior of its members is not firmly established.

Low turnover, and the regular and persistent pursuit of occupationally-specified careers, are among the conditions that must exist for thriving loyalties to specialized occupations and professions. Without question, these are less characteristic of nursing than of most professions, or, indeed, of many crafts. In common with many other fields of work, the demand for increased technological specialization in nursing may in fact alienate the professional and limit the scope of felt rewards to personal satisfactions from technical achievements.

Discussion

Dubin's major hypothesis was that work roles are assigned merely segmental importance in our society and that work is only one competing area of socially-patterned personal identifications. Hence, he concluded, work may be but little valued by labor-force participants. The results reported here suggest that his generalizations need amplification. At least in terms of the technique employed in this study, work appears to be a major, if not dominant, interest of the professional nurses who constituted our sample.

It remains to be seen whether other professionals, for example, in a field which is predominantly male, or in fields which typically involve independent practice such as optometry[5] or dentistry, reveal different patterns of preference for work locations. Unlike nursing, a dominant feature of such fields is the separation of work from a large organizational setting. The professional may work regularly with others such as receptionists and aides, both of whom he considers to be sub-professional. These are co-workers but not colleagues. At the end of a fatiguing work day, the professional optometrist or dentist may well prefer to relax with other people who are neither his non-professional work associates nor his professional peers. Responses to the "central life interest" inventory by these independent professionals might, as a consequence, show much less orientation to work than was evidenced by nurses.

Study of persons affiliated with other professions whose traditions do not stress independence from large organizations would provide an additional check on the results. Accountancy, where the major options appear to be employment in a department of a large corporation or affiliation with an accounting firm, or teaching, would be good examples of professions whose work occurs in organizational settings. In accounting, however, an historic ideal of independence has been taken over from the traditional ideology of small business ownership. Clinical psychology and social work are illustrative of the aspirant professions that have been tied in with organizational settings and have flourished and expanded in recent years as a direct result. A third interesting possibility is medicine, where hospitals provide large-scale settings for work. At the same time, that profession self-consciously asserts the independence of its members through the maintenance of separate offices, the vesting, in the hands of the medical societies, of critical power over hospitals, and the continuation of separate billing for professional services within hospitals.

Each of these several professions would be expected to have a somewhat different pattern. Medicine and accountancy have in common some tradition of independence in work. Accountancy appears to be less tenacious than medicine in using that tradition as the basis for the image of itself which it projects to the public. However, specialists in both fields usually perform their work in large and complicated organizational environments. It is probable that the unusual status concerns of physicians, coupled with their prestige and income, would result in a greater acceptance of work as a "central life interest" by them than by accountants.

In contrast, clinical psychology and social work have flourished within the context of large organizational settings and without the tradition of independence. Because of their fields' recent and very rapid growth, practitioners riding upon the success of these specialties might be expected to have intensive commitments to work and to their profession. Psychologists and social workers might be expected to show a greater concern for work than specialists in fields that have been stable for a longer period of time.

It may be appropriate to agree with Dubin's speculations that "the sense of attachment" to social organizations is a very important key to the understanding of contemporary industrial relations. For industrial workers, pride in work and in occupation may be less the center of personal identification than is pride in the organizations within the community to which they belong. In contrast to industrial workers, professionals still consider work and workplace as important and valued centers of their activity. Social relations within work settings are salient for professionals. Their specialized and prolonged training encourages the development of a commitment to work and to their professional community.

For industrial workers, mobility within the plant may mean a change from one level or type of job responsibility to another. Status within the factory implies interchangeability. Individuals cannot move easily from one profession to another, and advancements in rank as a professional generally involve merely a higher degree of responsibility in the same area of work. Within health institutions, however, the emerging emphasis on the "health team" may ultimately lead to the blurring of the separate identities of the participants from several related professions. The long-run consequence may be the loss by the individual professions of what Everett Hughes calls their licence and mandate.[6] If that occurs, one outcome may be the reduction in the professional's attachment to his profession and the rise in his attachment to the organization which furnishes employment as well as to groups outside the field of work. The pattern reported here may then be replaced, in part at least, by that reported by Dubin.

It is not surprising to find that many professionals prefer to derive their personal satisfactions from work and workplace. This is a component of the emerging self-concept encouraged during training, if not specifically dictated by it. Nor is it surprising to find that a greater proportion of professionals than of industrial workers prefer work as locus for informal social relations. Results for the items on technological behavior and participation in formal organizations are also in accord with the hypotheses. Organizations are critical features of the work lives of many professionals. These professional nurses structure formal organizational activity in terms of their work behaviors. Knowledge of the range of controls which constrain these nurses makes this result expected. Further, the emphasis during training and post-training stresses the learning and repetition of certain behaviors and activities considered to be at the core of the profession itself. Technological behaviors such as are covered in the questionnaire are not excluded in socialization for non-work roles but are obviously not important as a component of them.

In the final analysis, the "central life interest" inventory is a measure of values. When it is used to compare professionals and industrial workers, we learn something about the values of these groups. The professional nurses studied here, in contrast to Dubin's industrial workers, do have an overriding preference for work. However, it is not merely technology and competence in dealing with the technological components of the field that binds the professional to his work. The total value commitment by professionals is shown in the greater tendency for professionals than for industrial workers to situate informal group experiences, personal satisfactions and formal organization attachments within the work environment.

As the movement of specialties toward professionalization continues, and as more technical specialties make claims as professions, we might suppose that work will have greater implications for the performance of non-work roles. It might be argued that the more highly organized and professionalized such fields become, the more frequent will be the tendency for work roles to create demands that affect the patterning of non-work activities. Such demands may, however, slacken off as the specialty nears the professional model, and as the professionals can afford, in consequence, to relax.

Perhaps this can be the explanation for the 21 per cent of the nurses who did not portray work as a central life interest. These are the individuals who are unlikely to be dedicated professionals. This could be because of marital responsibilities, or beliefs that they will not remain within the field. However, the deviants may reflect upon a characteristic of the professional community in another sense. As mentioned above, professional fields may well vary in their capacity to have non-work roles of their specialists influenced by work requirements and professional obligations. The ability of these fields to constrain the behaviors of their participants may vary. Nursing as a field is apparently moving toward increased professionalization. The result may be increased constraint upon those who remain in the field, and as a consequent reduction in the amount of deviancy tolerated.

The differences between Dubin's findings for industrial workers and the current findings for professional nurses imply a greater commitment to work by these and perhaps other professionals. Many facets of the professionals' lives are affected by the nature of their work and the extent of their commitment to it and to their places of work. Work is obviously a highly valued, demanding and important feature of the many roles played in our society by professionals.

The professionals for whom work is a central life interest (not including lawyers) may consider participation in voluntary associations to be incompatible with their work obligations and an active involvement in community decision-making as an inappropriate and unnecessary use of time. Thus, they may withdraw or remain neutral on political issues. Such a disengagement can affect the level of public morality, as social power goes by default to others. In turn, sectors of the public may distrust the detached professionals and acutely resent even a rare venture into civic affairs. This view of professionals accompanies the belief that they ought to persist "until the work is done"; they *should* work more and harder than others; their satisfactions are not supposed to be primarily monetary. The underpayment of professionals, especially in fields where their associations do not significantly affect career entry or influence conditions of work, is a logical outcome.

Two circumstances suggest counterbalancing trends. One is the leveling effect on work roles of ubiquitous large-scale formal organizations. The contemporary professional is increasingly an "organization man," subject to job standardization procedures, personnel policies, and other structural coercions. His degree of participation in public matters may be much like that of other types of "organization man"; he may be resented as a member of the larger category of white collar workers, technicians and specialists. Second, professionals with deviant orientations to work may most readily come to the public's attention. The public may generalize to all professionals and believe them to be not very different from other categories of workers.

The outcomes of this study demonstrates the fruitfulness of recasting generalizations derived from the study of particular groups as hypotheses for further research under changed conditions. One prospective possibility is to duplicate the technique used in this and in Dubin's study with other work groups, thereby broadening our knowledge of the several ways in which participation in and commitments to work and work activity may affect the other role behaviors of occupational and professional specialists.

NOTES

1. Robert Dubin, "Industrial Workers' Worlds: A Study of the 'central life interests' of industrial workers," *Social Problems,* 3 (January, 1956), pp. 131-42. (Dubin's article also appears in this volume.)

2. See, for example, A. M. Carr-Saunders and P. A. Wilson, *The Professions* (Oxford: Clarendon Press, 1933).

3. Some minor changes in wording were necessary. Industrial terms, such as "the plant," were replaced by terms appropriate to the organizations where these nurses are employed. Otherwise, the instrument was the same as that used by Dubin.

4. Robert W. Habenstein and Edwin A. Christ, *Professionalizer, Traditionalizer, and Utilizer* (Columbia, Missouri: Institute for Research in the Social Sciences, University of Missouri, 1955).

5. Louis H. Orzack and John R. Uglum, "Sociological Perspectives of the Profession of Optometry," Reprint Series of the Industrial Relations Research Center, University of Wisconsin, No. 58/1, 1958.

6. Everett C. Hughes, "Licence and Mandate," in *Men and Their Work* (Glencoe: Free Press, 1958), pp. 78-87.

WILLIAM A. FAUNCE

Michigan State University

5

Automation and Leisure*

TWENTIETH-CENTURY WESTERN CIVILIZATION is confronted by at least one problem unique in human history. Man's historical preoccupation, working for the means of livelihood, is increasingly involving a diminishing portion of his time and energy. The problem of extracting from the earth the means of subsistence in an economy of scarcity has been replaced by a new set of problems in an economy of machine-made abundance. One such problem is the proper utilization of larger and larger amounts of available leisure time.

Many societies in the past have supported leisure classes of varying sizes with varying amounts of time free from productive activities. Leisure today is no longer the privilege of the few, however, but the prerogative of many. Never before has the question of how leisure time is to be used assumed such importance.

This new leisure as well as our economic abundance is machine-made, the product of the increasing mechanization of production technology. Spurred by the necessity of increasing productive efficiency during World War II, American industry appears to have entered another and perhaps unprecedented era of rapid technological change in production facilities. The term automation describes one direction which these changes have

---

* Reprinted by permission from *Automation and Society*, edited by H. B. Jacobson and J. S. Roucek (New York: Philosophical Library, 1959).

taken. In this article we will be concerned with the effect of automation upon amount of available leisure time, the effects of increased leisure upon patterns of use of leisure time, and the impact of an increasingly leisure-oriented society upon various American culture patterns.

Automation and Working Hours

The number of hours and days worked per week during any period tend to be regarded as natural and immutable. The five day, forty hour work week is currently so regarded. It has only been a decade or so, however, that this amount of working time has been the standard work week in this country. In the past century the average number of hours worked per week by non-agricultural workers has decreased from about sixty-five to about forty hours and this decline has been fairly steady, averaging about three hours per decade. As Seligman has noted,[1] it is the process of reduction of working time which appears to be "natural and immutable."

The increasing productivity of our economy is what has made this reduction in working hours possible. For the economy as a whole, output per man-hour has been rising by two to three per cent per year over the past fifty years. In the nongovernmental sector of our economy, output per man-hour has approximately doubled over the past twenty-five years. The benefits of this increased productivity have been distributed between income and leisure on roughly a 60-40 basis, 60 per cent going into greater income and 40 per cent for more leisure time. Whether this particular way of cutting the "productivity pie" will continue or not is difficult to predict. Some of the factors affecting the likelihood that automation will produce a further increase in available leisure time may be considered, however.

Examples of dramatic increases in output resulting from automation are legion. A chemical company has recently opened a magnesium mill which is capable of producing more magnesium sheet and plate than the total previous national capacity. A musical record company has installed new automatic machines with which four men turn out eight times as many records as 250 men had previously produced. An automobile engine part which was once produced at the rate of thirty-eight per hour by five men and two machines is now produced by one man at one machine at the rate of 750 per hour. One of the most highly automated automobile engine plants now produces twice as many engines with one-tenth of the manpower of a conventional plant. While hundreds of such instances might be cited, they are probably exceptional cases and automation has resulted in comparatively minor productivity increases in many plants and offices in which equipment of this kind has been introduced. However, the net effect of the development of rapid transfer machines, electronic inspection devices, and computer technology has undoubtedly been an increase in output per man-hour in American industry and has probably accelerated the rate of productivity increase.

The extent to which this increased productivity will be translated into shorter hours of work will probably be determined in large part by the amount of pressure brought to bear by trade unions and labor generally for reduced hours. The logic of cost reduction would, in most instances, dictate a management preference for longer hours and fewer workers when the point is reached at which a decrease in hours worked no longer increases productivity. This may be especially true where there are pressures to maintain continuous operation of expensive automated equipment in order to meet amortization deadlines. Thus far, a further reduction in the work week has not become an immediate collective bargaining objective of American trade unions generally. A number of unions, including the large, pattern-setting U.A.W., however, are committed to the shorter work week as a goal for collective bargaining and it seems probable that, with continued productivity increases, union pressure for decreased hours in other industries will follow.

Since the various industries within our economy are differentially susceptible to further mechanization, the possibility for decreasing hours of work may vary from industry to industry. Reductions in hours worked per week have occurred at varying rates in different industries in the past and will undoubtedly continue to do so. Because of the rate of change in production techniques and the likelihood that there will be greater pressure exerted to reduce the work week, it is probable that working hours of hourly rated employees in mass production industries will be among the first to be affected by automation. It is with these workers that this chapter is primarily concerned.

Relatively greater pressure to decrease the work week for production line workers may develop for a number of reasons. Automation appears to have already decreased the number of job opportunities available to such workers in some industries and, barring any great increases in product demand, seems likely to do so in others. Comparing the two year averages for 1947-48 and 1953-54 in the automobile industry, production workers increased 7.6 per cent, non-production workers increased 19.7 per cent, while total production increased 68.9 per cent. Semi-skilled operatives and kindred workers actually constituted a smaller proportion of the work force in 1956 than they did in 1947. In a recent study by the author, a majority of management representatives as well as of workers and union leadership in the automobile industry in Detroit expressed the opinion that automation would result in at least some short term displacement of workers. To the extent that automation results in reduced job opportunities, even in the absence of large scale displacement of workers, it is likely that there will be pressure exerted by unions to decrease hours in order to spread available jobs among a larger number of workers.

Changing standards regarding adequacy of style of life among working class families may also affect preferences regarding the distribution of income and leisure from increased productivity. Amount of income desired tends to be normatively regulated and there is some evidence that once a standard of living is established there may be less pressure to raise income than to maintain it at a customary level.[2] Demands for new goods and services are constantly being created by advertising campaigns and, more subtly, through models provided by the mass media and the consumption of many of these goods and services is dependent upon *both* greater income and more leisure. Many leisure activities which were once symbols of upper class status are now within the means of working class families and it is unlikely that the demand for more leisure time in which to enjoy these activities will slacken.

In connection with the study in the automobile industry previously mentioned, a sample of workers from an automated plant were asked whether they would prefer a shorter work week, increased wages, or longer vacations if any of these alternatives were made possible by automation. Almost three-fourths indicated a preference for a shorter work week over either more pay or longer vacations. One apparent reason for this preference is the very nature of production line work. Jobs of this kind have characteristically required little exercise of skill, responsibility, or initiative and have offered little variety in the types of tasks performed. Automation does not appear to have significantly altered these characteristics of production line work. Machine operators in the automated plant, while having somewhat more responsibility in that there is a larger machinery investment per worker, do not need appreciably greater skill and many feel that they have an even less important part in the total work process than had been the case in plants using conventional machining techniques. Neither does the change from actually operating a machine to pushing a button or watching a panel of lights or gauges offer much more relief from the monotony of repetitive operations on the job. In short, automation has not altered the fact that most production line jobs do not produce the kind of occupational involvement or identification necessary to make work a satisfying experience. If work is not a satisfying experience, it would seem reasonable to expect that there would be greater pressure to decrease working hours to allow more time for what may be perceived as more important and more satisfying activities.

There has not yet been sufficient research dealing with the factors affecting the preference of workers for greater leisure or more income to accurately anticipate the preferred distribution of the benefits of increased productivity from automation. It seems likely, however, that increasing productivity will continue to result in an increase in available leisure time. A majority of a sample of both union and management leadership in the automobile industry interviewed in 1957 expressed the opinion that there would be a reduction of working hours resulting from automation within five to ten years. It has been estimated that if the rate of productivity continues to increase at two or three per cent per year and assuming a continuation of the 60-40 ratio of distribution of increased productivity between income and leisure, a four-day work week may be feasible throughout the non-farm sector of our economy in twenty-five years.[3] For the manufacturing industries with which we are principally concerned, a shorter work week may be possible much sooner. If a change of this type does occur, the nature of leisure activities may be affected. There is evidence from previous research that the proportion of time spent in various activities increases or decreases depending upon amount of leisure time available.[4]

Patterns of Use of Increased Leisure

A number of dimensions of leisure activities may be considered in discussing the use of leisure time. Leisure may be recuperative in the sense that time is spent relaxing from the job completed and preparing for the job forthcoming or it may be actively spent in the sense of physical or emotional involvement in an activity. Leisure time may be used creatively or non-creatively. It may be self-oriented or may be other or service-oriented. It may be spent in the company of others or in solitary pursuits. It may be spent as a spectator or as a participant in various activities. Leisure time may serve as relief from boredom or as escape from involvement.

Automation may affect patterns of use of leisure time either by increasing the amount of time available for such activities or by changing the nature of the work experience. The combination of decreased physical effort required by automated jobs and decreased working hours would make possible a decrease in the proportion of time spent in recuperation from work and permit more active involvement in leisure pursuits. Since recuperative time is likely to be non-creative there would be at least the possibility for more creative use of leisure with increased time available. Production line workers desiring creative outlets would necessarily seek such experience in leisure activities because of the essentially non-creative character of work in either automated or conventional plants. Passive, recuperative time being primarily self-oriented, there would also be the possibility of an increase in service-oriented activities given more leisure time.

One of the effects of automation upon some types of production line jobs has been the social isolation of workers because of increased distance between work stations and increased attention required by the job.[5] Social isolation on the job may result in a larger proportion of leisure time being spent in activities involving others. This may be especially true for production line workers whose occupational roles do not encourage "self esteem testing" on the job so that recognition of success is more likely to be sought from colleagues in leisure activities. For this reason it is also likely that, given sufficient leisure time to acquire skills adequate to insure some measure of success in these activities, workers may spend a larger proportion of leisure time as participants in activities rather than as spectators.[6] Finally, it follows from the preceding discussion of the nature of automated jobs and the relation of work and leisure that for production line workers, leisure activities are more apt to function as relief from boredom than escape from involvement. For any occupational group in which work is seen as a means rather than an end in itself, leisure is less likely to represent freedom from involvement than it is freedom to become involved.

There has been almost no research measuring *directly* the effects of increased leisure upon patterns of use of leisure time. There have been a number of studies in which workers in mass production industries have been asked how they *might* use increased leisure if it became available. The accompanying table is an example of the findings from one such study. The activities listed are those indicated as things a group of workers from an automated automobile engine plant would like to do if they had either longer vacations or a shorter work week. Research involving actual situations where working hours are reduced for workers in automated plants would be necessary to test hypotheses regarding the impact of automation upon leisure activities. The results of this study suggest, however, that automated production line workers may spend a larger proportion of increased leisure time as active participants with others in activities that are potentially creative and service oriented. The data reported in Table 1 will be referred to in the concluding section of this chapter where some possible consequences of increased leisure for American culture are considered.

Some Broader Implications of Increased Leisure

The possibility that automation may increase the amount of leisure time available to large segments of the population of industrial communities has perhaps broader implications than any other of its potential consequences. In the event of a shortening of the work week there would be an obvious need for expansion of community recreational facilities. Another and

TABLE 1

Proposed Use of Increased Leisure Time

		Per cent of Workers Listing Activity N = 125
1.	Work around the house	96.8
2.	Spend more time with family	76.8
3.	Travel	53.6
4.	Go to ballgames, fights, hockey games, etc.	48.8
5.	Fishing and hunting	42.4
6.	Other hobbies	25.6
7.	Engage in some form of athletics (bowling, golf, baseball, etc.)	24.8
8.	Read more	24.8
9.	Go back to school or learn a trade	19.2
10.	Be more active in school boards, P.T.A., boy scouts, etc.	17.6
11.	Get another part time job	16.8
12.	Join more social clubs	15.2
13.	Engage in more political action work	12.8
14.	Rest, relax, loaf, etc.	11.2
15.	Swimming, boating	4.8
16.	Work on car	2.4
17.	Church activities	1.6

more important example of the effects of greater leisure upon community facilities may be its implications for the schools. The data in Table 1 suggest that almost twenty per cent of the workers interviewed would, with more leisure time, go back to school or learn a trade. If anywhere near twenty per cent of just automobile workers decided to go back to school, existing facilities in many communities would be inadequate to meet increased enrollments. As the application of automated machinery to production in other industries becomes more common and if a shorter work week results, the problem would become even more acute.

A more important long range problem posed by increased leisure for the schools, however, may be the necessity of including within the curriculum training for the creative use of leisure time. While there is already a growing emphasis in American education upon training for citizenship in the community and a de-emphasis of vocational training, it may be important for curriculum planners to recognize that the citizen in the automated industrial community may have an increasing amount of leisure time at his disposal. Automation may require that there be more adequate provision made for training in certain kinds of technical skills as well, but, in the long run, the primary responsibility of the schools may well become that of instilling certain kinds of values and interests which permit the creative use of leisure and, in general, the teaching not of vocational but of leisure skills.

Increased leisure produced by automation may also have an affect upon the role of the local union in community power structure. If automation reduces the size of the work force in the automated plant, the number of grievance proceedings and other day to day union-management relations as well as the number of most other functions usually performed by the local union may also be expected to decrease. It is the testimony of history, however, that power once held is only reluctantly relinquished and, that, while institutional *structure* may be slow to change, the *function* of various structural units may vary more readily. If it becomes no longer necessary for the local union to perform its various traditional functions at the plant level, it may well turn with increasing interest to participation in community affairs. The local union, or in larger communities, the regional councils representing various locals, may, for example, become increasingly involved in political action at the community level. Approximately thirteen per cent of the automobile workers interviewed indicated that with more leisure time they would be interested in engaging in more political action work. If this figure is at all representative of the general interest of industrial workers in becoming active participants in political affairs, local union leadership would have little difficulty in finding volunteer workers in sufficient number to wage an effective political campaign in most communities. Increasing involvement of local unions in community politics would be consistent with the increasing interest of the A.F.L.-C.I.O. in political and social action at the state and national levels and might in some communities, produce significant changes in community power structure.

Agencies outside the local community would also be affected by a shortening of the work week. The proportion of workers indicating a desire to spend more time hunting and fishing suggests that state conservation department activities may need to be considerably expanded. It may also be necessary for highway and expressway planners to take into account the effects of changing technology upon working hours. A system of roads designed to accommodate a peak traffic load composed primarily of work trips may be inadequate to handle the traffic which may possibly enter and leave industrial areas on weekends if a shorter work week results from automation. Well over half of the workers interviewed indicated that with more leisure they would more often engage in activities that would necessarily take them out of the city.

It seems probable that a further reduction in working hours might also produce changes in patterns of family relationships in American society. Seventy-eight per cent of the workers interviewed in this study indicated that with greater leisure they would spend more time with their families. Ninety-eight per cent of the workers indicated that they would, with more leisure, spend more time working around the house. Leisure which need not be used as recuperative time may be spent by the industrial worker in more active participation in family activities. With the worker in the home for longer periods of time, he may take a more active role in the socialization of his children, a function currently performed very largely by the mother in American families. The current process of transition from a partriarchal to an equalitarian authority structure in the American family might also be affected by an increasing involvement of the father in family affairs.

The number of possible consequences of an increasingly leisure oriented society for American culture which might be discussed is limited only by the span of years considered and the scope of one's imagination. The examples considered above are only a few of the potential effects of increased leisure suggested by the data presented in Table 1.

There is one broad question of values regarding leisure not yet considered. It has been assumed that the choice of alternative benefits from increasing productivity will be between increased personal income and increased leisure. There is a third possibility. An increased national income might be used to provide services not adequately performed at present. While it seems obvious that we are becoming an increasingly leisure oriented society, it is not nearly so apparent that we *should* become so. The increased national product resulting from a continuation of the present pattern of working hours plus increased productivity from automation might be used to provide funds for hospitals, schools, and other service agencies but, perhaps most importantly of all, for research in the social, physical, and life sciences.

The "age of atoms and automation" is nearly upon us and the magnitude of the decisions occasioned by its approach becomes increasingly apparent. The conflicting values inherent in the possibility of alternative cultural orientations toward leisure or service require the careful consideration of decision-makers in American society.

NOTES

1. Daniel Seligman, "The Four Day Work Week: How Soon?",
Fortune, (July, 1954), p. 81.

2. Bakke has noted, for example, that among working class
individuals one is regarded as successful when he has attained the
standard of living customary among his associates. E. Wight Bakke,
The Unemployed Worker (New Haven: Yale University Press, 1940),
p. 20.

3. Daniel Seligman, *op. cit.*, p. 114.

4. See, for example, George Lundberg, *et al.*, *Leisure* (New York:
Columbia University Press, 1934), p. 123.

5. W. A. Faunce, "Automation in the Automobile Industry: Some
Consequences for In-Plant Social Structure," *American Sociological
Review*, XXIII (August, 1958).

6. A recent study by Alfred Clarke suggests that our current
concern with "spectatoritis" in American leisure patterns may be
unwarranted. Alfred C. Clarke, "The Use of Leisure and Its Relation
to Levels of Occupational Prestige," *American Sociological Review*,
(June, 1956), pp. 304-5.

ROLF MEYERSOHN

State University of New York at Stony Brook

6

Changing Work and Leisure Routines*

IN JANUARY, 1958, a small aircraft-parts manufacturing company changed its work routines. On the basis of a decision made by its management in late 1957, the work schedule was altered so that during one week in every month the plant would operate from Tuesday to Saturday instead of the usual Monday to Friday. This revision was intended to give the employees a three-day weekend every month without a reduction in the total weekly number of hours worked.

This minor alteration offered the Center for the Study of Leisure a unique opportunity to study two important problems. In the first place, it provided a chance to find out how easily routines of work and leisure can be modified; that is, how willing people are to change their habits. This question seemed particularly important in view of the fact that identical work and leisure routines for a large majority of the American population have created enormous problems of overcrowding and overtaxing recreational and transportation facilities. A shift in the schedules for some would mean better use of limited facilities for all.

The second problem, more easily identified and studied as a result of this alteration in the work schedule, is that of attitudes toward leisure. Most social phenomena are difficult to study

* I am indebted to David Riesman for assistance in the development of this study, an earlier version of which was delivered at the Fourth World Congress of Sociology, Milan-Stresa, Italy, September, 1959. The reseach was supported by the University of Chicago Center for the Study of Leisure.

97

because they are typically routine and undramatic. Leisure, for example, is a category of life which tends to be taken for granted, to which certain chronic attitudes are brought, and which, despite the ideals held out by western society for the active "pursuit of happiness," tends to be identified and distinguished primarily in a negative way—as the absence of work.

The shift in time and habit brought on by a change in the work schedule was thought to be potentially dramatic enough to make those involved more aware of their own attitudes toward work and leisure. The employees here were in effect making a new *social contract* in which they agreed to "give" a Saturday to their work in order to "receive" a Monday. (It might be noted that some of the workers felt that this "installment plan" was less satisfying than a scheme whereby they might "work now and pay later"—that is, work one Saturday in order to earn a day off subsequently.)

The plant studied is located in southern California, a region perhaps more self-conscious about leisure than other parts of the United States. For a variety of reasons its residents appear to give more emphasis than Americans elsewhere to the various comforts and enjoyments of life. Many originally settled in southern California because of its benign climate and some were undoubtedly attracted by its many recreational facilities. Even the fact that the "New Calendar" (as the changed work schedule was labeled by the management) was instituted here and not elsewhere might be taken as a reflection of this leisure orientation.

For the purposes of this research, such a bias—if it exists—is not disturbing; instead it might even be expected that the kinds of attitudes and sentiments found in California are symptoms of what might prevail in other parts of urban America in the future. If this New Calendar is successful here it might be adopted elsewhere; if it does not work in southern California, it is likely not to work anywhere else.[1]

The aircraft-parts plant is located in Torrance, California. According to a special census taken in 1957, the population of Torrance is 93,000. In 1950 it was 22,000. This increase is a striking one, although in southern California (again unlike most of the rest of the nation), such growth is considered normal. Torrance is an industrial town despite the suburbanization represented by the population growth figures, and modern plants are found alongside equally modern single-family housing developments. It has several post offices, two local biweekly newspapers, several motels (no hotels!), and a multiplying number of schools and shopping centers. Yet, in the remarkably traditionless traditions of southern California, Torrance melts into the sprawling landscape of an area known as South Bay, which extends from Los Angeles to Long Beach.

This study, then, examines workers in South Bay area, rather than in Torrance. The employees came from all over the area; some lived as far as thirty miles away; a few lived across the street. Over 90 per cent drove to work, most in their own cars. A very small number could walk to work. No one traveled to work by means of public transportation: there was none.

Two weeks after the first three-day weekend (which included New Year's Day and hence was not a unique experience), self-administered questionnaires were distributed among all 465 employees, asking them to report their attitudes toward the New Calendar, their activities on the free weekend, their plans for future weekends, attitudes toward their jobs, and background information. Seventy-nine per cent returned usable questionnaires. A second questionnaire was given in July, after workers had six months' experience with the New Calendar.

Unfortunately, the year 1958 happened to be a very poor one for industrial research of this kind, not to mention industrial employment. This plant, like most others, suffered from a recession, and while in January there were 465 employees, by July they numbered only 188. Whatever experiences workers had with this New Calendar, they were deeply affected by the recession; hence, this report cannot provide an indication of how such a plan might work out in normal times. To trace attitudes about this plan over an extended period of time was made difficult in part because of the enormous reduction of the population under study (and of the sample, aggravated by the fact that in July only 50 per cent returned the questionnaire), in part because the employees who "survived" grew less concerned with problems of rearranging their work schedule and more concerned with having one at all.[2]

Even though the New Calendar was imposed by management, rather than arrived at through any kind of mutual consent,[3] it was very widely accepted by the employees, as Table 1 indicates. As a matter of fact, over half the respondents thought that they would like the plan more as they became accustomed to it, and only 5 per cent thought they would like it less.

In its releases to the public and the employees, the company had announced that the New Calendar was instituted to provide an opportunity for its employees to go on longer trips. When the employees were asked why they favored the plan, most mentioned this possibility, and some thought this free day would also provide time to carry out various home projects and chores for which the rest of the week never seemed to provide enough time.

The only disadvantage that could be anticipated was having to work on a Saturday. Some employees thought it would be better if the company could find an alternative, ideally if they could simply grant a four-day week once a month, or at least permit workers to make up for the free Monday by night work. (Management could consider neither plan seriously, however; the first was not feasible because the company could not afford to cut production without cutting costs—though some workers claimed that their productivity could easily be stepped up if

TABLE 1

Attitudes toward the New Calendar in January, 1958

"How do you like the New Calendar?"	Percentage
"I like it very much."	49
"On the whole I like it."	29
"Don't care one way or other."	7
"On the whole I dislike it."	11
"I dislike it very much."	3
No answer	1
Total per cent	100
Number of respondents	369

there were such an incentive; as for nightwork, this would have had to be paid at overtime rates.) Working on Saturdays was seen most negatively by female employees (20 per cent of the work force), who had husbands and children to take care of when they came home. However, in January at least, the temptation of free Mondays more than offset these disadvantages in the eyes of most of the employees.

As was indicated earlier, it was generally expected that the change in the work schedule would be even better liked later on; presumably it would be most popular in the summer, when children are out of school and the weather more inviting.

Such expectations were hardly borne out. Table 2 shows the attitudes toward the New Calendar reported in July.

It should be pointed out again that the number of employees shrank from 465 to 188, and the number of respondents from 369 to 99, twenty of whom were hired since January, and hence cannot be included in any direct change analysis.

A comparison of Tables 1 and 2 indicates that between January and July a considerable drop occurred in the popularity of the New Calendar, from 78 per cent to 56 per cent expressing a preference for the New Calendar. Table 3 demonstrates that this increase in the proportion disliking the plan was not due to any accidental (or deliberate) difference in the rate of lay-offs among those who were favorably inclined in January; in other words, the change did not occur because the company laid off a

TABLE 2

Attitudes toward the New Calendar in July, 1958

"How do you like the New Calendar?"	Percentage
"I like it very much."	27
"On the whole I like it."	29
"Don't care one way or other."	10
"On the whole I dislike it."	22
"I dislike it very much."	10
No answer	2
Total per cent	100
Number of respondents	99

TABLE 3

Attitudes toward New Calendar in July 1958 Among Those Who Answered the Question in January, 1958

"How do you like the New Calendar"

		January "I like it very much" & "I like it"	All others	Total
July	"I like it very much" & "I like it"	66%	13%	56%
	All others	34	87	44
Total		100%	100%	100%
Number of respondents		62	15	77
Percentage of respondents		80%	20%	100%

larger number of positively inclined employees. Rather, the increase in the dislike came as a result of changes in the attitude on part of those who were initially favorable.

Very few who initially disliked the New Calendar changed their minds, but one-third of the initially favorable employees grew to dislike the New Calendar. Why? Unfortunately the influence of the recession cannot be measured, and there is no way of knowing whether or not under normal circumstances a similar drop might have occurred. The July interviews make clear, however, that the shift in attitude was due to negative experiences with the three-day weekends, and these in turn could be related to the recession. In January, the plan had been popular because employees expected to do interesting things on their free Mondays. But over the next months, most of them did very little (perhaps because of the recession and the general tightening of budgets, perhaps because in general prospects might be more attractive than realities), and by July there was much less to be enthusiastic about.

Several interrelated changes occurred, which will be discussed separately.

1. *The Recession.* Southern Californians generally and people associated with the aircraft industry specifically—so it seemed to me when I administered the first wave of interviews—have a

particularly well-defined self-consciousness about growth and prosperity. Looking back over the past decade, comparing their own present circumstances with their past, reading the local newspapers concerning the glorious prospects about the future, following the ever-growing waves of inmigration rates and programs of construction—in other words, partaking of what seemed like a permanent boom—this group of workers experienced a considerable shock when in the spring of 1958 the first serious reversal set in. In other areas, more used to the ups and downs of industrial society, there are undoubtedly a number of cushions built into the social structure; but here, the recession was a disaster. As a matter of fact, when I tried to interview some of the employees who had been laid off I had a hard time finding them, so many of them had gone "back home," to the South, the Southwest, and the Midwest.

The respondents reported on here are the survivors. Most were apprehensive about the future, and a general mood of pessimism was reflected in their attitudes. Approximately two-thirds (63%) of the employees thought that they had a good chance to get ahead in their particular occupation, only 43 per cent that they had a chance with their company.

Most studies of unemployment, such as the classic Jahoda, Lazarsfeld, Zeisel *Die Arbeitslosen von Marienthal*,[4] naturally focus on the effects of unemployment on the unemployed, and little attention has been paid to the surviving workers. The present study—which was not designed for such emphasis—suggests that some similarities exist between the "still-employed" and the unemployed. Earlier studies had determined that the unemployed make few plans for their leisure (if it can be called that), are unlikely to do anything special in their free time, and if unemployed long enough tend to become apathetic and despondent. Elements of these traits were found among the employed workers who replied to the July questionnaire. They are discussed below.

2. *Planning for future weekends.* In January workers could not yet have had any disappointments with the New Calendar, since it had not been tried. But by July there were many. When asked in January what plans they had for future

weekends, approximately half the respondents replied that they had some plans, such as traveling, or being with the family, or doing some shopping or some chores. In July, it turned out, many who had made plans did not realize them, for reasons which are not altogether clear, but which can be partly attributed to the recession. For example, one respondent reported in July that he had planned to go camping for the Fourth-of-July weekend, but decided that he had better save the gasoline expenses.

Even more important than carrying out the plans that are made seems to be planning itself. While in January half the respondents reported plans for future weekends, in July only a third said that they had any plans. In both time periods, planning is strongly related to attitudes toward the New Calendar, as is seen in Table 4.

The increasing tendency to refrain from planning for future leisure is striking—and reminiscent of studies of the unemployed—particularly in view of the fact that the summer is usually the time for weekend activities.

3. *Redefinition of the New Calendar.* In January the only complaints vented against the New Calendar centered around working Saturdays. This grievance increased considerably, since presumably the necessity of having to work on a Saturday is

TABLE 4

Attitudes toward New Calendar by Planning, January and July, 1958

| "How do you like the New Calendar?" | Do you have anything special planned for future months? | | | |
| | January | | July | |
	yes	no	yes	no
"I like it very much." "I like it."	92%	66%	79%	47%
All others	8	34	21	53
Total	100%	100%	100%	100%
Number of respondents	173	193	28	68

worth while only if something interesting or exciting had taken place over the preceding three-day weekend. Otherwise one "pays for services not rendered."

But in addition, a new complaint was voiced, namely, against the free Monday. A number of men and women reported in July that they did not enjoy having Monday off because there was nothing to do. To a large extent, the free Monday was actually used for home chores, if at all, and these could usually be carried out as easily on Saturday. With wives at work and children at school, the Monday seemed for a number of the men to turn into rather lonely occasions, without even the relief of television—which on weekdays is designed almost exclusively for women and children. It is interesting to note that those who favored the New Calendar were likely to consider the free Monday as part of the weekend, while those who did not like it thought of it as a separate day—possibly an "indigestible" period of time which could not easily be incorporated into the rest of their lives. The extent to which the recession had anything to do with such attitudes is not known.

Another new definition of the New Calendar, perhaps the most interesting one, is a complaint never mentioned in January, namely, the feeling that there was no respite for ten days; the employees worked from one Tuesday until the following Friday with only one day off. It is significant that of the many ways in which the New Calendar *could be perceived,* this definition became the most common one. Instead of considering the potential advantages with respect to leisure, workers increasingly saw the plan in terms of its disadvantages with respect to work.

Only a small number of workers admitted that they had been bored on their free Mondays. But over half thought that they might be bored on future Mondays. It is possible that people are more likely to fear boredom than to experience it. But equally possible is the alternative that in the continued absence of clear ideas on how future free time will be spent, the anticipation of boredom could turn into reality.

Postscript. In November, 1958, the employees voted, by a two-to-one majority, to discontinue the New Calendar.

NOTES

1. For further discussion of this point, see David Riesman, "Leisure and Work in Post-Industrial Society," in Eric Larrabee and Rolf Meyersohn eds., *Mass Leisure* (Glencoe, Ill.: The Free Press, 1958), p. 369.

2. Needless to say, the decision of management to institute the New Calendar had nothing to do with the recession; at the time there was no indication that any layoffs would be made.

3. The plant had no union.

4. Allensbach and Bonn: Verlag für Demoskopie, 1960.

HAROLD L. WILENSKY

University of Michigan

7

The Uneven Distribution of Leisure: The Impact of Economic Growth on "Free Time"*

IN THEIR SEARCH for the shape of the modern social order, many students have pointed to the steady drop in average hours of work—the emergence of what is variously labeled "the new leisure" or the consumer-oriented society. In advertising parlance, we are moving from the "Fabulous 'Fifties" to the "Soaring 'Sixties," in which the average man will wallow in an abundance of "free time" (and the goods and services to fill it). Sometimes the point of comparison is Reformation Europe, more often some decade of the 19th century. A typical formulation: from 1850 to 1950 we moved from a 70- or 72-hour workweek down to a 40-hour week—a 12-hour day, six-day week to an eight-hour day, five-day week, or we have increased our free time—beyond work, eating and miscellaneous necessities—from about 2.18 hours a day in 1850 to 7.48 hours in 1960.[1] It is usually assumed that hours of work will continue to decline. (In 1955 a 20th Century Fund study predicted a 36.5-hour week by 1960; the 40-hour standard still prevails, but union agitation for more leisure continues.)

Whatever their judgment of the quality of the new leisure,

---

* Reprinted from *Social Problems*, Vol. 9, No. 1, Summer, 1961.

and whatever their explanation of the main drift, most ob-
servers assume that economic growth brings a rather heavy drop
in the propensity to work. This idea rests on time series for
various societies and industries which show that increased
productivity is negatively correlated with hours of work; and
cross-sectional studies by economists of earnings and hours,
which again show a strong negative correlation.[2] Orthodox
economic theory distinguishes two effects of a rise in hourly
earnings—*an income effect* (people can afford to buy more
leisure) and a *substitution effect* (leisure costs more in foregone
income). But the theory does not say which will predominate;
we have only the empirical findings coupled with assumptions
about the taste for leisure or leisure as a "superior good."

Sociological explanations of such data emphasize the impact
of rising income on leisure styles: increased preoccupation with
consumption, more stable family life, the diffusion of middle-
class, suburban participation patterns—a general withdrawal from
work and an intensified search for substitute leisure commitments, with concomitant changes in social stratification and
political life.[3]

Discussion of these matters suffers from too limited a time
perspective and from data which fail to capture important
variations in the propensity to work among men variously
situated. This paper argues that while the affluent society may
foster an underlying preference for leisure, the emerging structure of opportunity means that a growing minority works very
long hours while increasing millions are reluctant victims of too
much leisure. I will review evidence regarding trends in hours
of work and leisure, and then report data on the choice between
income and leisure among selected occupational groups and
strata. In the sense of hours not worked for pay or profit, who
has most and least leisure? How are leisure hours distributed
over the day, the year, the life cycle? In what way are these
hours "free" or "voluntary"?

Trends in Amount of Time Worked

Here, as in all talk of the changing human condition, much
depends on the places and times to be compared and the

quality of the data. The data are weak, but certain tendencies appear likely.

1. *In the perspective of several centuries, time at work increased before it decreased.* The secular decline in hours and days of work is greatly exaggerated by the usual comparison of gross daily or weekly averages with those of the "take off" period of rapid economic growth in England, France, and America—a time of horrendous working schedules and conditions. Estimates of *annual* hours and days of work for populations of *earlier* times yield less confidence in great progress and surely suggest the absence of a unilinear downward trend in the past several centuries.

Among the citizens of antiquity, as well as among primitive agriculturalists, the number of days of leisure often approached half of every year. The transformation of tabooed or unlucky days into holy days, and the latter into holidays—what an early student of the matter calls "man's ineradicable tendency to convert his fast days into feast days"[4]—occurred long before the middle ages. "In the old Roman calendar, out of 355 days, nearly one-third (109) were marked as . . . unlawful for judicial and political business."[5] In the last two centuries of the republic, festival days were stretched to accommodate more spectacles and public games. The Roman passion for holidays reached its climax in the middle of the fourth century when days off numbered 175. If we assume a 12-hour day, which is probably on the high side, total working time would be only about 2,160 hours a year. Whatever the work schedules of slaves and women, leisure for the ruling classes, for administrative and professional men, was never again so abundant. Hours of work for comparable populations in subsequent centuries seem to have increased sharply. Fourastié estimates that French "intellectual" workers in courts, ministries, and administrative agencies worked about 2,500 hours per year in 1800, 3,000 to 3,500 in 1950.[6] In short, historical materials suggest a considerable loss of leisure for higher strata through the ages, although lower white-collar men (e.g., office messengers, clerks, notaries) have gained since 1800.

What about farmers and urban workers? The problem of estimation for both is the rhythm of the seasons and the day.

Estimates for traditional European agriculture put annual hours
at 3,500-4,000 throughout the early period; this did not change
until the twentieth century.[7] For urban areas, while daily
schedules of 12-16 hours are reported as early as the thirteenth
century (after the emergence of flourishing commercial cities
in the West), the number of days off and the record of one- or
two-hour lunch periods and half-hour breaks suggests that annual
hours were little more than they are for a fully employed worker
today.

According to a basic sourcebook on work rules in thirteenth-
century France, night work, Sunday work, and work after
Saturday vespers (4 to 5 P.M.) were forbidden in most trades,
although some privileged artisans were exceptions to these rules.[8]
In many trades (e.g., tapestry-makers in Beauvais) the 12-hour
day include a half-hour rest in the morning and an hour at lunch.[9]
Craftsmen such as wire-drawers in Paris received 30-day vacations in addition to the normal 141 days off; they worked only
about 194 days a year—a 16-hour day in "summer" (six months),
an eight-hour day in "winter" (six months).[10] The total: 2,328
annual hours.

TABLE 1

Only About Half of the Labor Force Works Year-Round Full-Time[*]

Type of Worker	Per Cent of Persons Who Worked in 1957
FULL-TIME WORKERS (35 hours or more per week)	81.0
Year-round full-time workers—worked primarily at full-time jobs for 50 or more weeks during the year	55.1
Part-year full-time workers—worked primarily at full-time jobs for less than 50 weeks but more than 26 weeks	15.5
Intermittent workers—worked primarily at full-time jobs, but for 26 weeks or less	10.4
PART-TIME WORKERS (less than 35 hours per week)	19.0
Year-round part-time workers	6.4
Part-year part-time workers	12.6

[*] D. J. Bogue's summary of U. S. Bureau of the Census' Annual survey
of work experience. *The Population of the United States.* Glencoe, Illinois:
The Free Press, 1959, p. 453.

From the late middle ages to 1800, the drift in manual occupations was unmistakably toward longer hours. Dolléans and Dehove report workdays in the city crafts of 14 to 18 hours.[11] And the number of days off declined from the fifteenth century on.[12] By 1750, day laborers were working perhaps 3,770 hours.[13] By 1850 the average workweek in French cities was about 70 hours,[14] and some estimates put it higher.[15] The record of daily and weekly hours for England is similar—e.g., a climb from a 12-hour day with a two-hour rest in 1700 to a 14-18-hour day in 1800,[16] when the stage was set for humanitarian protest against the costs of industrialism.

The burden of labor in our century, of course, has lessened;[17] today annual hours are down in the range 1,900-2,500—a return to the work schedules of medieval guildsmen.

2. *Recent increases in leisure have been unequally distributed by industry and occupational category.* Most of the real gain in leisure in the U. S. has come to private nonagricultural industries—especially since 1850—and most markedly in manufacturing and mining, and to agriculture in the last 50 years, especially since 1940. Professionals, executives, officials and other civil servants, and the self-employed have benefited little, and in some occupations have lost out. In such industries as all-year hotels, buslines and local railways, and telegraphic communications, the workweek did not drop below 44 hours until the 1950's.[18]

This disproportionate leisure gain in manufacturing and mining, and recently agriculture, is given emphasis by statistics on seasonal and part-year occupations. Table 1 shows that about one in five of those who worked in 1957 worked primarily at part-time jobs; one in ten, at full-time jobs, but 26 weeks or less; one in six, 26-50 weeks.

The part-timers and intermittent workers are heavily concentrated among women, non-whites, young workers, old workers, and rural workers. And the concentration by occupation is striking: a full year's work is typical of white-collar people—salesmen, clerks, proprietors, managers, officials, and professionals (excepting female teachers). But in 1949 only about half the laborers (farm and non-farm) and female operatives

worked the full year; only three in five of the private household
workers and male operatives had a full year.[19]

This picture must be modified slightly by the longer voluntary
vacation of upper strata. Table 4 shows that men who work
very long hours tend to take long vacations. This is especially
clear among professional groups (short-hours short-vacation
engineers vs. long-hours long-vacation lawyers and professors)
and older white-collar workers.[20] But the main outlines none-
theless stand up. For instance, if a year-round full-time professional takes a four-week vacation and works about 2,400 hours
per year (50 hours a week for 48 weeks) for only 40 years,
his worklife total (96,000 hours) will still exceed that of the
year-round full-time blue-collar worker who takes a two-week
vacation, and works about 2,000 hours (40 a week for 50 weeks)
for 47 years (94,000 hours). Since the blue-collar man seldom
works year-round full-time, lifetime leisure seems heavily
weighted toward the lower strata. Low-status jobs held by a
majority of the labor force have shown the fastest drop in the
workweek; they also provide more weeks off per year.

3. *Despite an increasing age of entry into the labor force and
a decreasing age of exit, men today work more years over the
life cycle than they did in 1900.* The fraction of the total life
span worked, however, has changed little—because of increased
longevity. Again there are crucial differences among occupational
strata and groups. Tables of working life show that in 1900 the
average labor force member who was twenty years old could
expect to live another 42 years, of which only three would be
retirement years. In 1950 his life expectancy was forty-nine
years, of which nearly six would be spent in retirement. Length
of working life has gone up about 15 per cent, length of retirement has doubled.[21]

But look at the variations by occupational category in Table 2.
There is a correlation of −.82 between the quality of occupations
(indicated by earnings and education) and the mean length of
working life.[22] Clearly, men in better jobs spend less of their
lives working. Variations on the main theme: extremely arduous
or hazardous jobs (e.g., mining) bring very early retirement or
death, while many professionals never stop working—they fade

away, like old soldiers, pencils in hand. For reasons of both motive and opportunity (including job-linked health factors) the truck driver or the man on the assembly line, if he lives on, will sever his work ties earlier and more completely than the professor or physician.[23]

4. *While the labor force participation rate for women increases with economic growth, the trend by occupation is away from long-hours jobs,* such as domestic service and farm labor, into shorter-hour jobs, such as sales and clerical.[24] Whether this means more "leisure" for women is another matter; typically, work is added to traditional housewifery, and female *work*life expectancy is going up at a faster rate than life expectancy or non-working years[25]—with a dubious net result, as we shall see on the following page.

In sum: If we begin with either antiquity or Europe before the Reformation, average hours of work per year, if not per week, moved upward into the nineteenth century. The twentieth century decline in work has been grossly exaggerated by selective comparison with the shocking schedules of early English textile mills—an episode which dominates historical discussion of the evils of industrialism.

Moreover, the daily or weekly averages obscure important inequalities in the distribution of leisure. With economic growth the upper strata have probably lost leisure. Professionals, executives, officials, and proprietors have long workweeks, year-round employment. Their longer vacations and shorter worklives (delayed entry and often earlier retirement) do not offset this edge in working hours. Although life-time leisure decreases with increased status, the picture is one of bunched, predictable leisure for elites whose worklives are shorter; and intermittent, unpredictable, unstable leisure for the masses, whose worklives are longer.

A Portrait of Long-Hours Men

On the assumption that the quantitative and qualitative barriers to the leisure-oriented society could be better grasped if the most and least leisured groups were more precisely located, I have compared long-hours men with other men in several

TABLE 2

On Average Higher Strata Work Fewer Years Than Lower Strata[*]

Major Occupational Category	Mean Number of Years in Working Force	Average Age of Entry	Average Retirement Age
Professional, technical and kindred workers	40 years	Late	Early
Managers, officials and proprietors, except farm	41	Late	Early
Craftsmen, foremen and kindred workers	44	Late	Average
Operatives and kindred workers	45	Early	Early
Sales workers	47	Early	Average
Clerical and kindred workers	47	Early	Average
Farmers and farm managers	48	Late	Late
Laborers, except farm and mine	51	Early	Late
Farm laborers and foremen	52	Early	Late
Service workers	52	Early	Late

[*] Source: A. J. Jaffe and R. O. Carleton, *Occupational Mobility in the United States,* 1930-1960 (New York: Columbia King's Crown Press, 1954), pp. 49-50. "Mean number of years" summarizes occupational differences in rates of new entries and retirements as of 1950; it is a synthetic figure, since few men spend their entire worklives in the same census category. The results are similar for 1940 and 1930. The actual distribution of employed older workers in 1959 as reported by M. S. Gordon shows a similar picture, but suggests later retirement for managers, proprietors, and officials. "Work and Patterns of Retirement" in R. W. Kleemeier, ed., *Aging and Leisure* (New York: Oxford University Press, 1961), pp. 19-20. The variations within this category are large. See Table 4 below.

samples ranging from upper-middle class professionals to high-income operatives.

Samples and Methods. The analysis is based on detailed interviews with probability samples or universes of six professional groups and a cross-section of the "middle mass" in the Detroit area, stratified for comparability with respect to age, income, occupational stratum, and other characteristics. Interviews were done in the first half of 1960. Selection criteria applied to all were: white, male, members of the labor force, married now or in the past. All the professionals had college degrees. For lawyers and engineers additional criteria were applied in an initial phone contact to screen in the eligibles; personal selector interviews were used for the middle mass; the universe of eligible professors was interviewed. The special criteria:

1. *Lawyers.* Selected randomly from the Michigan State Bar Roster and the Martindale-Hubbell Law Directory. Age: 30-55. Family income: at least $8,000 in one of the past five years. All have law degrees and derive half or more of total income from law.

a) *Solo lawyers.* A pure type including only individual practitioners or two-man family partnerships in the Detroit area. May be associated with other lawyers but does not share clientele on any permanent basis.

b) *Firm lawyers.* Selected from the 19 Detroit firms with ten or more partners and associates. House counsel were excluded.

2. *Professors.* Full-time faculty of arts and sciences colleges in two universities. Rank: assistant professor and up. Age, 29-55. Disciplines: physical sciences (including mathematics) and the humanities. Excluded: the social sciences and professional schools. Both institutions are large, but not eminent.

a) *"Church U."* Church-controlled.

b) *"Urban U."* A fast-growing state university.

3. *Engineers.* Had an engineering degree or its equivalent. Age: 30-55. Family income: at least $8,000 in one of the past five years. Generally research and development specialists, supervisors, or executives. Two large enterprises:

a) *"Unico."* A unit making one main product subject to great fluctuations in demand. Reputation: a dead end for engineers.

b) *"Diversico."* A unit with diversified operations, and a history of stable growth. Reputation: recruiting ground for top executives in central headquarters.

4. *The middle mass* (lower-middle class and upper-working class). Selector questions bracketed in men, aged 21-55, whose family incomes in any one of the past five years reached $5,000 or more but never topped $13,000. The upper-middle class was excluded by use of a list of ineligible occupation-education categories based on authority and skill. Occupations which re-

mained—clerks, salesmen, craftsmen, foremen, small proprietors, semi-, marginal- or would-be professionals and technicians, managers and officials with few subordinates, and operatives with high income—constitute the core of the metropolitan middle mass.[26]

The questions used to estimate "usual weekly hours" and "choice" are indicated in table footnotes.[27]

Findings. The most striking result is the sheer number of hours these men work:

Usual Weekly Hours (all jobs, all days)	Combined Samples (1168)	Middle Mass Only (678)
Under 40	6%	6%
40-44	35	40
45-49	16	14
50-54	14	11
55-59	8	7
60 or more	16	14
Unemployed or NA	5	8
	100%	100%
Usual Week-end Hours		
None	20%	22%
1-8 hours	56	48
9 or more hours	18	20
Unemployed or NA	6	10
	100%	100%

About half put in 45 hours or more per week; a sizeable minority work at least 60 hours. One in five works more than a full day on weekends. One in ten currently holds a spare-time job; one in three has been a moonlighter some time in his work history.

Who are these eager beavers? Detailed analysis of the 24 per cent who log 55 hours or more a week sheds light on their propensity to work.

Table 3 shows that a third of the high-income men in the combined sample work at least 55 hours a week compared to about a fifth of the less affluent. (Finer breaks below $10,000

TABLE 3

Men With High Family Incomes More Often Work Long Hours*

| Usual weeklyhours | Total Family Income, 1959 | | | | | | | |
| | Under $10,000 | | $10,000 and over | | NA or unemployed | | Total | |
	%	N	%	N	%	N	%	N
55 or more	19	135	31	135	21	6	24	276
Fewer than 55	74	521	67	292	69	20	71	833
NA	7	47	2	9	10	3	5	59
Total	100	703	100	436	100	29	100	1168

* The questions follow. For middle mass, lawyers, and engineers: "Now some additional questions about your present job. You said you are a (SPECIFY MAIN JOB). How many hours a week do you usually work at this job? What time do you usually start and stop work on a regular weekday? Counting both Saturday and Sunday, about how many hours do you generally put in on a weekend?" For all samples, a battery on moonlighting picked up extra hours; for professors, there were additional questions on hours spent in standard activities, as well as consulting.

show no differences.)[28] Other social attributes, however, may be more important. Column 1 of Table 4 summarizes variations in the portion of each occupational group or category usually working 55 hours or more. There is a general tendency for higher occupational strata, like the high income men of Table 3, to work long hours. But the differences *between* strata (e.g., 13 per cent between all professions and low manual workers of comparable age) are not nearly as large as the differences *within* strata (e.g., 28 per cent for solo lawyers vs. Diversico engineers). At every level, there is a group or category where about a third work at least 55 hours—lawyers, professors, lower-middle class managers, upper working-class youngsters. Only about a fifth of all lawyers and one-fourth of the professors work *fewer* than 45 hours per week while about one-half of the engineers and middle-mass work that little. This again emphasizes that often what looks like "class" phenomena may be rooted in more specific work milieux, career patterns and organizational contexts, as well as ethnic and religious subcultures.[29]

TABLE 4

Per Cent of Occupational Groups and Strata Usually Working at Least 55 Hours Per Week by Various Social Characteristics°

	Work 55 hrs. or more	Work 55 hrs. or more and Control own work sched.	Education		Fam. inc. $10,000 and over	Per cent of worklife self-employed			Religion				4 or more weeks vacat.
			Some college	Less than H.S.		Never	1-39%	40-100%	C	P	J	NP	
Total Professional	28% (490)	22 (490)	28 (490)		31 (321)	23 (302)	42 (60)	32 (128)	28 (117)	24 (283)	44 (54)	37 (35)	41 (76)
Solo Lawyers	38* (100)	30 (100)			40 (75)	0 (0)	60 (20)	32 (80)	30 (33)	33 (30)	49 (35)	50 (2)	47 (17)
Urban U. Professors	37 (68)	34 (68)			28 (36)	38 (65)	0 (3)	0 (0)	29 (7)	36 (28)	25 (12)	50 (20)	44 (23)
Church U. Professors	36 (31)	26 (31)			58 (12)	37 (30)	0 (1)	0 (0)	38 (26)	0 (2)	100 (1)	0 (2)	36 (11)
Firm Lawyers	29 (107)	21 (107)			32 (95)	14 (28)	35 (34)	34 (45)	30 (20)	27 (77)	50 (6)	25 (4)	45 (20)
Unico Engineers	24 (91)	17 (91)			29 (58)	24 (89)	50 (2)	0 (0)	25 (12)	25 (76)	0 (0)	0 (3)	0 (1)
Diversico Engineers	10 (93)	8 (93)			11 (45)	10 (90)	0 (0)	0 (3)	5 (19)	10 (70)	0 (0)	25 (4)	0 (4)
Total Middle Mass, Family Income $5,000 to $13,000	21 (678)	9 (678)	23 (176)	22 (243)	31 (115)	15 (515)	33 (105)	50 (56)	20 (309)	20 (313)	43 (23)	16 (31)	23 (44)
Total White Collar, Age 30-55	27 (251)	16 (251)	25 (109)	43 (56)	39 (62)	15 (165)	46 (43)	55 (42)	24 (109)	25 (115)	47 (15)	46 (11)	43 (16)
Small Proprietors	59 (59)	36 (59)											
Managers	33 (43)	16 (45)											
Semi-professional	14 (88)	10 (88)											

The following table is printed sideways on the page. Each cell shows a percentage working at least 55 hours a week, with the base number (n) in parentheses below it. The two columns nearest the group labels carry entries for every group; the remaining columns carry entries only for the four summary (Total / Grand Total) rows.

Group	% (n)	% (n)											
Other Low Non-manual	12 (61)	7 (61)											
Total White Collar, Age 21-29	23 (69)	16 (69)	21 (33)	46 (11)	50 (6)	21 (53)	33 (9)	29 (7)	25 (28)	23 (35)	25 (4)	0 (2)	50 (2)
Small Proprietors	33 (6)	33 (6)											
Managers	50 (10)	20 (10)											
Semi-professional	19 (27)	11 (27)											
Other Low Non-manual	15 (26)	15 (26)											
Total Blue Collar, Age 30-55	14 (304)**	9 (304)	21 (28)	13 (158)	17 (40)	12 (246)	21 (52)	20 (5)	14 (140)	15 (144)	50 (4)	0 (16)	4 (24)
High Manual	14 (220)	2 (220)											
Low Manual	15 (73)	7 (73)											
Total Blue Collar, Age 21-29	24 (54)**	2 (54)	0 (6)	22 (18)	29 (7)	20 (51)	100 (1)	100 (2)	28 (32)	21 (19)	0 (0)	0 (2)	50 (2)
High Manual	31 (36)	3 (36)											
Low Manual	12 (17)	0 (17)											
Grand Total Middle Mass and Professionals	24 (1168)	14 (1168)	27 (666)	22 (243)	31 (436)	18 (817)	36 (165)	37 (184)	22 (426)	22 (596)	44 (77)	27 (66)	34 (120)

* Read all percentages as the portion of the group working at least 55 hours. For instance: 38 per cent of the 100 solo lawyers work at least 55 hours. Going across row two, 60 per cent of the 20 solo lawyers who have spent 1-39 per cent of their worklives in self-employment work at least 55 hours a week. Data on men who work less than 45 hours are reported in the text where relevant,

** Total includes all the unemployed in all these samples—12 men of the middle mass.

The propensity for certain groups to work nineteenth-century factory hours is sharpened if the individual member has had some experience in self-employment, or is Jewish, or both. High income has a slight and consistent effect across the groups; education and age have erratic but still interesting effects. Entrepreneurship is a powerful impetus to long hours. Leading the long-hours rates are small proprietors (59 per cent log at least 55 hours) and solo lawyers (38 per cent).[30] Complete work histories enabled a classification of all respondents by portion of years in the labor force spent in self-employment. Among men who spend up to two-fifths of their worklives in self-employment, 33 per cent work long hours; a longer time in self-employment yields 50 per cent. The trend is accounted for mainly by the lower white-collar workers, aged 30-55. Professionals work long hours most often when they have experienced both salaried- and self-employment. The 55-hour rate reaches a whopping 60 per cent for those solo lawyers who have in the past worked in bureaucratic contexts—a reflection perhaps of their deviant careers (they are late starters struggling to build a new practice, accountants, real-estate salesmen, or claims adjusters switching to law and trying to carry clientele with them when they set up shop on their own, etc.). Even among lawyers now in firms, a previous taste of self-employment puts many in the mood to chalk up long hours.

What about religion? The "Protestant Ethic," if it flourishes anywhere in these samples, flourishes among the Jewish professionals and white-collar workers; Catholics and Protestants, while they are unevenly distributed among occupational groups, are virtually identical to each other in their propensity to work.

High income, again, does not remove the drive to work; it slightly but consistently boosts the 55-hour rates for the occupational groups in Table 4—especially for white-collar strata.

Education, which is unrelated to hours of work by itself, has an unexpected effect when combined with occupation. While a taste of college increases the long-hours rate for older blue-collar men, it depresses the rate for younger blue-collar workers. Most important, failure to complete high school is an impetus to hard work among lower white-collar men—about half put in at least 55 hours. The *under*-educated white-collar men apparently have to knock themselves out to achieve and maintain their position. The *over*-educated working-class youngsters, analysis shows, are all intergenerational skidders with chaotic work histories—downward mobile men retreating from work.

Do the long-hours men prefer their way of life or are they forced into it by the nature of their work? If having control of one's own work schedule and working at least 55 hours is taken as an indicator of preference for income over leisure, then most of these men have such a preference. Table 5 shows that men who control their schedules more often work long hours than men on fixed schedules, especially among those with incomes under $10,000. And Table 4 pinpoints the types—the reluctant drudge and the ardent puritan. Compare column one (the long hours rate) with column two (the per cent of the total who worked long hours *and* control their own schedules). The greater the difference, the more men there are whose hours are more-or-less beyond their control. The big discrepancies—15 per cent or more—appear for small proprietors (older ones, since the youngsters are too few to talk about), lower-middle managers, and young blue-collar workers (men who, from other evidence, tend to feel squeezed on and off the job). The other groups, especially the professionals, semi-professionals, and young salesmen, clerks, etc. ("other low non-manual") more often work these hours by choice.

It is tempting to note the professional and white-collar totals and conclude that since these categories in the labor force are growing relative to the shorter-hours manual workers, the propensity to work is increasing. But the variations among groups give one pause. Chart 1 is an attempt to assess the net outcome; it takes these small samples as symbolic of larger populations whose size and projected rate of growth of decline can be estimated. "Long-hours" groups are those in which the per cent working at least 55 hours exceeds the average for the combined samples.

If we consider only the urban male labor force, the chart lends mild support to the general argument thus far: long hours for vanguard groups is a concomitant of continued economic

TABLE 5

Men Who Have Control of Their Own Schedules Work Longer Hours Whatever Their Income*

Usual weekly hours	Total Family Income, 1959																		
	Under $10,000						$10,000 and over						NA or unemployed		Total	
	Fixed sched.		Controls schedule		Sched. NA		Fixed sched.		Controls schedule		Sched. NA					
	%	N	%	N	%	N	%	N	%	N	%	N	%	N	%	N
55 or more	15	71	28	63	7	1	20	34	38	100	20	1	21	6	24	276
Fewer than 55	79	368	67	51	15	2	77	129	60	159	80	4	69	20	71	833
NA	5	24	6	13	77	10	3	5	2	4	0	0	10	3	5	59
Total	99	463	101	127	99	13	100	168	100	263	100	5	100	29	100	1168

* "Thinking now of your schedule of work—the hours you put in—do you have much control over this, or is your schedule more or less fixed?"

growth. Taking account of farmers, however, there would actually be a decrease in the propensity to work (i.e., the portion of long-hours men in the total male labor force would decline for the decade). Since farmers are a rapidly-declining long-hours group and will approach an irreducible minimum, probably after 1970, shifts in the composition of the labor force will take place mainly within non-farm occupations—where the net outcome gives an edge to the long-hours groups. Of course, any projection based on so many judgments is hazardous. Moreover, these estimates of long-hours rates draw only on selected segments of the labor force where family incomes top $5,000 (samples reported above).

Finally, consider the freedom to set one's own schedule and note the underlying preference for short hours among upper blue-collar workers now working long hours. Here the outcome would be reversed; a retreat from work would be widespread. Without a full analysis of the economic aspirations and expectations of the entire population, we cannot dismiss the hypothesis that there is a growing *desire* for more leisure, whatever the quantitative constraints imposed by the occupational structure.

The Illusion of "Free Time"

Time is more than astronomical and quantitative; it is social and qualitative.[31] An hour does not seem the same to all people everywhere. Units of time acquire quality and meaning from the beliefs and values and the routines of life that prevail in society.

In every society men perform the tasks, economic and non-economic, that fall to them by virtue of their social position. But the notion of "free time," time set aside and unconstrained, is a peculiarly modern idea; in the primitive tribe or peasant village, work is hardly distinguished from the rest of life—from one's duties and rights as husband, son, father, clansman.[32] Having conceived of the idea that time off work is free time, industrial man proceeds to define such time as one of the great benefits of economic growth. In order to arrive at clues to the quality of these added non-work hours, let us examine again those who have most leisure and those who have least, now

CHART 1

Long-Hours Men May Be a Growing Minority of the Non-Farm Male Labor Force

Vanguard Groups and Categories						Rearguard Groups and Categories					
Long Hours (25% or more work 55 hrs. or more)	1950*	1970**	*Short Hours* (less than 25% work 55 hrs. or more)	1950	1970	*Long Hours* (25% or more work 55 hrs. or more)	1950	1970	*Short Hours* (less than 25% work 55 hrs. or more)	1950	1970
Urban U. Profs. Church U. Profs. Firm Lawyers (bureaucratic professionals, intellectuals)	1.5	2.3	Engineers Semi-professional (fast-growth scientific, technical employees)	4.8	10.8	Solo Lawyers (indep. prof.)	1.0	1.1	Low Blue-Collar Operatives	20.1	17.1
Lower White-Collar Workers, esp. Managers, Officials, and Men with High Income. (growing middle bureaucracy, part-college-educated)	5.3	10.6	Other Low Non-Manual			Self-Employed esp. Small Proprietors (Non-prof. entrepreneurs)	5.4	4.9	Service (Excl. protective, etc.)	5.4	6.5
			Clerical	6.4	7.4				Laborers (Excl. farm and mine)	8.1	5.7
			Sales	6.4	7.0						

	Young High Blue-Collar or High-Income Blue-Collar (Skilled craftsmen, foremen, etc.)		Older High Blue-Collar (Craftsmen, etc., protective serv.)			
	7.3	8.0	11.9	12.7	6.4	6.0
TOTAL	14.1	20.9	29.5	37.9	33.6	29.3

* Estimated per cent of male labor force in 1950.

** Projected per cent of the male labor force in 1970. Based on guestimates of the size in 1950 and projections to the early 1970's of the 1950-61 rate of growth or decline of the categories opposite one another. Procedure: Examine census detailed occupational composition of the civilian male labor force in 1950. Bogue, *op. cit.*, pp. 522-36. Fit these to the categories in parentheses above. E.g., estimate the distribution in 1950 of "Professional, technical, and kindred" (7.3% in 1950) among established bureaucratic professionals (1.5%), solo professionals (1.0%), putting what was left in engineers and semi-professionals (4.8%). Use as a guide the actual per cent increase 1940-50 in detailed occupational categories (*Ibid.*, pp. 479-82), and changes in the per cent of the male labor force in major occupational groups from 1950 to April, 1961 (computed from *Ibid.*, pp. 522-36, and *Bureau of the Census, Employment and Earnings,* 7 [May, 1961] Table A-10, p. 6). Now project the category's fraction of the labor force to 1970. (E.g., engineers, technicians and semi-professionals—short-hours vanguard groups—are more numerous and will likely grow faster than the established bureaucratic professions listed to their left.) Repeat for all categories. Net result:

	1950	1970	Net change
Long-hours groups	20.5%	26.9%	+6.4%
Short-hours groups	63.1	67.2	+4.1
Farm men	15.2	5.9	—9.3

bringing into view the old as well as the young, the poor as well as the affluent.

Men Condemned to Leisure: The Forced Withdrawal from Work. The best clue to the nature of the "new leisure" is the fact that leisure became defined as an urgent social problem in the Great Depression, when we witnessed the largest universal reduction in working hours ever achieved in the United States. Those who have most leisure are typically reluctant victims: (1) the involuntarily retired, (2) the intermittently unemployed, (3) the chronically unemployed—all growing categories of the population.

Since 1890 there has been an accelerating decrease in the labor force participation rates of men in Great Britain, Canada, Germany, New Zealand, and the United States. Men aged sixty-five and older have reduced their participation rates far more than any other age category. The main reason for this withdrawal from work among the aged is declining opportunity.[33] Reduced opportunity is a function chiefly of:

1. *Educational and occupational obsolescence.* Employers are reluctant to retain or hire older men when stronger, better-trained, and often less-costly personnel are available. Much of the displacement of older men has been due to the increased availability of middle-aged women for clerical, personal service, and professional jobs and young high-school and college graduates in all fields. From this flows:

a) Compulsory retirement policies and age discrimination in hiring. As Long says, these practices were common decades ago, but there is clear evidence that they are more likely to prevail in larger firms—and an increasing fraction of the labor force works in such firms. Also, if concern over unemployment increases, and is intensified by the rising rate of new entrants, union sentiment for imposing or lowering compulsory retirement ages will grow.

2. *The decline of "old men's" jobs in proportion to the number of old men.* Older workers are concentrated in occupations that are dying out or declining—farmers, blacksmiths, tailors, locomotive engineers.[34] The number of guards, doorkeepers and watch-

men is not increasing as fast as the number of elderly men who
want such jobs.

Do older workers retire not only because they lack opportunity,
but because they prefer leisure? A desire for leisure could express
itself if both financial security and health among the aged were
at high levels, but this test has not come. The evidence, while
not conclusive, points (as in the past) to ill health as the main
reason for "voluntary" retirement, and income as the main reason
for staying on full-time.[35] At least in the short run, as opportunities decline, the number of men who want to go on working and
cannot is likely to increase.

The partially unemployed and the chronically unemployed
in all age categories perhaps account for more life-span leisure
hours than any group except women. Job insecurity under the
most prosperous conditions is common. In 1957, when the
national rate of unemployment averaged only four per cent, at
least 15 per cent of persons who worked at some time that year
experienced one or more episodes of unemployment.[36] We have
already seen the high incidence of part-time work (Table 1).
While much of this is involuntary, some of it is no tragedy—the
partially-retired professional, the housewife or student with a
spare-time job, the moonlighter with two jobs. Chronic unemployment is another matter, and it is becoming more acute. An
increasing number of people are condemned to leisure by the
changing economic structure. Unemployment is concentrated
among low-status service workers, and unskilled and semi-skilled
manual workers in construction, manufacturing and trade (they
are disproportionately very young, elderly, non-white or foreign-
born). Growth in these labor-force categories has been slower
than growth in all categories other than farming; an accelerated
decline in most of these jobs is in the offing. Meanwhile, the
reproduction rate of these workers, at least in the recent past,
has been on the high side. Moreover, a very large fraction of
the numerous children of the less-skilled do not acquire the
training and ability, information, and motivation to break out
of the poverty circle. An old paradox becomes more prominent:
those whose productivity is highest will work longer hours partly

to support the forced leisure of men rendered obsolete by the activities of long-hours men.

What about time available to the more fortunate—men with steady jobs? We have already seen that many are busy choosing income over leisure. Is it because work itself becomes more free? Is the working population increasingly mixing business and pleasure?

Long-hours Men at Work. A new romanticism has crept into recent social analysis of work. Instead of a glorification of the medieval craft life (coupled with an attack on dehumanized labor), we now hear that work is becoming more like play.[37] Machines and incentive systems that permit men to work ahead and then loaf, union contracts providing call-in pay, standby pay, paid rest and lunch periods (as well as paid holidays and vacations, sick leave, and other leaves), the long coffee break among white-collar girls, the lunch "hour" among top business and professional people, card games among night-shift employees, shuffleboard on the floors of California aircraft factories—the illustrations are apt, but they may obscure central tendencies.

First, the total man-hour equivalents for all types of leave for production and related workers in manufacturing in 1958 were only about six per cent of the total hours paid for.[38] Even a liberal estimate of official and unofficial breaks on-the-job would not bring the whole (paid absences plus "leisure" in the workplace) to more than 10 per cent of the year's work routine.[39]

Second, recent technological changes mentioned above are likely to break up many informal workgroups that now soften the impact of formal rule and impersonal discipline. The British union which asked for "lonesome pay" for workers in a newly automated plant is symptomatic.[40] Clerical girls whose extended coffee breaks irritate the boss give way to office machine operators whose work is less flexible; the sales clerk who joins his colleagues to control the bonus and reduce sales-grabbing gives way to extra managers, floorwalkers, and checkout cashiers in self-service establishments; the paternalistic office manager is displaced by the IBM 650 and its ancillary personnel, whose frivolity is confined to feeding instructions to the machine so that it prints out "I have processed all data. I hope you have liked my work." Too much of the sociological picture of work comes from a few case studies of small job shops with man-paced machines—where men whose ingenuity in transforming work into play, while out-foxing the boss and his time-study man, will be constrained as industry continues its truly Weberian rationalization.

Third, the elites, who, it is said, cannot distinguish work from leisure and whose expense accounts are said to symbolize the Good Life, may stick to business more than we think. One breakdown of average hours of business executives shows about 43 hours at the office plus seven hours doing paper work and business reading at home. These 50 hours *exclude:* "business entertaining" at home (2.6 hours), the journey to work (5.3, including some reading and conferences en route), combined business-social functions outside the home (2.8) and a variable number of hours in business travel.[41] Even the long lunch period is something of a myth, if we can believe *Fortune's* microscopic dissection of the executive life: engagement pad analysis showed an average time of 1½ hours.[42]

Finally, the view that the reduction of drudgery in modern work has also meant a less disciplined performance of tasks and the injection of a playful atmosphere in the workplace mistakes the variety of experience of our rural forebears. It is true that the seventeenth century was a grim age for the colonists; their belief that pleasure was an offense in the sight of the Lord served their survival needs. But things relaxed a little only a hundred years later:

> Training days when young men prepared themselves for the business of war, became community holidays. Bees of various kinds transformed into frolics the building of houses, the husking of corn, or the preparing of fruit for drying. "I have never been so happy in my life," wrote Crèvecoeur in the eighteenth century, "as when I have assisted at these simple merriments, and indeed they are the only ones I know. Each returns home and is satisfied, and our work is done."[43]

The leisure of the upper classes, of course, followed that of the English gentry—especially on plantations of the South

(George Washington was an enthusiastic follower of the hounds). And the long-hours predecessors of President Kennedy apparently found time for a bit of fun on the side. Here is an extract from the note-and-expense book of Thomas Jefferson for the three weeks—June 10–July 2, 1776, during which he was drafting the Declaration of Independence:[44]

Lost at backgammon	7/6
Won at backgammon	7d 1/3
Won at cross and pyle	3 3/4d
Mrs. J. lost at cards	1/3
Lost at lotto	18/.

A return to sterner ways of life came in the first half of the nineteenth century, when the 14-hour day and the "wholesome discipline of factory life" were defended by preacher and employer alike as a deterrent to drunken leisure among urban workers, a view not entirely rejected by organized labor itself.[45] Even in the full swing of early industrialism, however, inhabitants of the Satanic mills had their moments of play. Historians have noted both a familial and a communal atmosphere in English factories of the eighteenth century and even those of the 1830's —ceremonial whiskey feasts when a spinner "changes his wheels, or gets new wheels," new hands standing a round of drinks as a token of goodwill, new masters doing the same, and, paradoxically, personalized supervision of children and relatives by parents, all working in the same mill.[46]

Whatever the trend in the mixing of business and pleasure, tales of the effort to make more tolerable and free time freer should not obscure two striking changes in the character of modern working time: (1) a more disciplined ordering of the sequence and timing of tasks; (2) more fragmentation and inflexibility of daily and weekly work schedules.

The economic order of the few advanced societies is something new: never in history has so large a portion of the working population been subject to so many formal social constraints in its economic activity. The time clock, the plant rules, the presence of a host of supervisors and other control specialists, the close attention to quantity and quality of output—these add up to a demand for discipline on the job, and acceptance of individual responsibility for job performance. We half forget the sustained regularity insisted upon in office, store, and factory —we are so used to it.[47] This increased discipline fits a well-known sociological formula: the more specialization, the more interdependence; the more interdependence, the greater the cost of failure to meet role requirements, and the greater the resources devoted to keeping men in line; the more complex the society, the larger fraction formal rules is of all rules (the mores and folkways give way to laws and by-laws) and the less tolerance for ambiguous social structures. We see this in such diverse facts as the correlation between policemen as a per cent of the labor force and size of community, and a recent tendency to routinize administrative and technical tasks by use of "information technology"—computers, mathematical programming and operations research—the beginnings of a revolution in middle bureaucracies.[48]

Three short-run trends will increase the accent on disciplined work routines among those fully employed: (1) The composition of the tertiary sector, now more than half the labor force, is shifting toward the less "free" occupations. E.g., the largest and fastest-growing professions are bureaucratized—engineers, technicians, scientists, professors, social workers, nurses, teachers. And in retail trade, as in manufacturing, the number of planners, supervisors, schedulers, expediters, and co-ordinators is growing. (2) Part-time workers aside, there is a large and growing number of people who have claims on the economy without working—students, the aged, the chronically unemployed. This should intensify an already urgent demand for education, health, recreation, welfare, and other services. (3) Scarce service and control specialists, like physicians in the past, will feel compelled to work long hours on tight schedules, whatever their changing vacation patterns. For one thing, their work time will be so valued that leisure will be an increasingly costly choice.[49] In any case, Table 5 shows that those who have freedom to set their own work schedules tend to choose long hours.

We see, then, that much of the modern gain in "free time" is illusory. Most leisure is forced leisure; and work becomes

more disciplined, not more playful. Even the leisure hours of
steady workers may become constrained by two structural facts:
the bunching of leisure under conditions of population boom,
and the inflexibility of work schedules.

The Bunching of Leisure. For the majority of adults, leisure
over the day, the week, the year, indeed, the life cycle, tends
to be bunched. While about half the gain in leisure since 1900
has been taken in shorter daily hours, several facts point to an
underlying preference, where leisure is to be had, for its greater
concentration: the two-day weekend, the spread of premium
penalties for Saturday and Sunday work, the growth in the
number of holidays, and the rapid increase of paid vacations,
especially two-week vacations. The union push for the shorter
workweek, which is prompted mainly by the desire to spread
scarce work, will likely result in a modest reinforcement of
existing patterns—more holidays (i.e., occasional four-day weeks),
an extra week's vacation geared to seniority (some industries
already have four weeks for those with 20 years' seniority).
Many union people think that workers would rather have such
leisure-bunching than the shorter workday:[50] for the family-
bound, long vacations and occasional long weekends enable
them to fix up the house, spend time with children, etc.; for
others, such periods permit hunting, fishing, or other trips; for
all, the pattern provides leisure when everyone else has it.

Whatever workers want, leisure bunching generally suits the
convenience of American employers. It is less costly and easier
to schedule than a flat reduction in the workweek or workday.[51]

Leisure bunching may *not* suit the convenience of modern
totalitarian societies. For instance, there are some signs that
Soviet planners prefer the shorter workday to its alternatives.[52]
The Soviet press is full of puritanical complaints about dancing,
drinking, and jazz; it adopts an aggressively educative tone in
all characterization of "rest" (the word leisure is seldom used
except for humorous or archaic effect[53]). "The reduction of the
working day," says one Soviet ideologue, "will release a
tremendous amount of strength and energy. . . . And people
will . . . study the sciences, production, they will be busy
inventing, rationalizing."[54] "Free time," says another, "is by no

means time for idling. In his leisure hours the advanced Soviet worker rests, studies, takes up the arts, sports, etc. Proper use of free time, by helping to develop the individual in all directions, becomes a powerful stimulus to production and higher labor productivity."[55] Such articles are peppered with attacks on the mistaken notion that leisure will be squandered in entertainments and amusements.

It is likely that the short workday reflects Soviet preoccupation with economic growth. It permits skilled workers to teach vocational school at night,[56] and all workers to hold second jobs and participate in continuing education or community projects. The long weekend or vacation, in contrast, encourages fishing trips or just plain loafing. Mr. Khrushchev may mean to bury us in an onslaught of moonlighting, paid and unpaid.

Totalitarian and pluralist societies alike may find one scheduling trend in common: more men on deviant schedules. For various reasons it pays to adopt continuous operations in the most advanced manufacturing industries (e.g., oil refining, chemical, paper, steel, cement) and in the growing tertiary sector (e.g., entertainment and recreation, protective service, communications, transportation, distribution). These industries require evening and night work. It is possible that the ten to twenty per cent of the labor force now on second or third shifts will increase.[57] Now, few men like odd shifts.[58] And the idea that no one should be stuck with a poor shift permanently often means rotating shift work (moving to a new shift every few days, months, or on the half year). A maximum fragmentation and inflexibility of the leisure routine may be the result. Time seems more chopped up; and the chance to stylize leisure in the most varied ways is reduced (many activities and associations are precluded, few are opened up).[59]

A Parkinson's Law for Women. No discussion of trends in the number and quality of leisure hours can avoid consideration of those who have the most apparent choice in the matter. For women the law is, "work expands so as to fill the time available for leisure." A paradox shows the law in action: *Female labor force participation rates have soared as impressively as male rates have dropped. Yet females exert most pressure for shorter hours.* Declining household and child-care responsibilities, rising educational levels, coupled with the retention of traditional housewifery, have transformed women into a labor supply ideal for several segments of modern economies. The deviant schedules and part-time jobs in the tertiary sectors, the nurturant and subordinate professions, psychologically akin to female family roles—women fit in very well, indeed.[60] They want a shorter workday because emancipation, while it has released them for work, has not to an equal extent released them from home and family. French students of leisure, drawing on their long tradition of time-budget and consumption studies, have given us a realistic estimate of this situation. Table 6 shows a breakdown of hours spent in housework, child-care, and paid labor among urban married women.

The female "workweek" is surely as long as it was a century ago. *"Plus ça change, plus c'est la même chose."*

Does the greater mechanization of the American home and our more efficient system of distribution lighten the burden of the American housewife? Despite talk of "outdoor housekeeping" in suburbia, the new burden of more elaborate home maintenance, the running and repairing of machinery, and an increase in financial management, physical drudgery has surely been reduced—both for housewives and their teen-age daughters. Labor-saving devices, more light and heat, better safety and health, speedier transportation and communication—these have doubtless cut back the minimum number of hours necessary to maintain the home. The resulting free time, however, is filled by work (especially at the two peaks of labor force participation—twenty to twenty-four and after forty), the recent increase in number of children, and an infectious rise in consumer expectations that keeps women busy on the shopping front. The quality of the remaining leisure is a matter of speculation.

Moreover, if employers and workers continue to prefer an orthodox bunching of leisure, the present transportation-communication overload should increase sharply—which could hit working housewives more than their spouses. Most women work mainly for income to support families or to supplement their husband's income and thereby boost consumption and

A *Contemporary Social Problem*

Table 6

*French Urban Housewives–In the Labor Force or Not–Have a Long "Work" Week**

	Hours on Job, Job Travel	Household Activities Excluding Child-Rearing	Child-Rearing	Total Hours of Work Per Week
Working Wives				
No children	51	27	....	78
One child	45	32	8	84
Two children	37	36	11	84
Three or more	34	39	11	84
Non-Working Wives				
No children	....	55	....	55
One child	....	53	17	70
Two children	....	56	19	75
Three or more	....	55	23	78
All Wives				
No children	36	35	....	71
One child	26	41	11	78
Two children	14	49	15	78
Three or more	9	50	20	79

* Based on Table XIII, pp. 606-7 of Alain Girard, "Le budget-temps de la femme mariée dans les agglomerations urbaines," *Population,* 13 (October-December, 1958), pp. 591-618. Averages are from daily time budgets kept in five-minute units by 1,020 married women under forty-seven years old. Sample: 84 French urban areas with populations above 5,000. "Household activities" includes: cleaning, etc., shopping, cooking, dishwashing, sewing, and gardening (which, in average time, were negligible). "Child-rearing" includes: physical care of babies, watching children at home, taking them for walks or to school, supervising school lessons and other duties, medical care. Excluded from "work": sleep, eating, personal care, entertainment and rest in and out of home, religious practice, and "helping husband in his work" (n.f.s.).

enhance leisure. The transportation squeeze makes a full-time job more difficult; women are reluctant to commute long distances.

Scheduling trends affect more than the journey to work. Increasing standard leisure for some necessitates deviant hours for others—or a decline in the amount and quality of the leisure services received by the majority. Service workers have recently won *shorter* hours; it is not clear how much pressure they will exert to avoid *deviant* hours. While many supermarkets and suburban shopping centers stay open evenings and weekends, some do not, and curtailment of service is common in repair shops, stockrooms, parts depots, clinics, libraries, and museums.[61]

It seems possible that a growing population, with a preference for bunched leisure and insatiable appetites for services, will escape to the suburbs to avoid congestion, and then spend its leisure commuting and waiting—hanging on the phone, standing in line, cruising for parking space. Any service overload tends to thwart the consumption aims of women's work and reduces time for family life.

Conclusions

The average man's gain in leisure with economic growth has been exaggerated. Estimates of annual and lifetime leisure suggest that the skilled urban worker may have gained the position of his thirteenth-century counterpart. Upper strata have, in fact, lost out. Even though their worklives are shorter and vacations longer, these men work many steady hours week after week—sometimes reaching a truly startling lifetime total.

Are the long-hours groups in the vanguard or rearguard? The variations within traditional categories for which data are reported make predictions of the future propensity to work very difficult. Considering both occupations which *necessitate* long hours (proprietors, some young skilled workers and foremen) and those in which men *choose* to work hard (professors, lawyers), there appears to be a slowly-increasing minority of the male urban labor force working 55 hours a week or more. If we consider only those who control their own schedules, the short-hours men would carry the future—with the middle mass of moderate means and moderate inclination to work dominating the scene.

On the question of quality: modern work is disciplined; process and product, timing and sequence of tasks have never in history been so explicitly prescribed. Modern leisure, while it becomes more rigid and fragmented for a growing minority comes bunched in standard packages for most people (in America a response to both employer and worker preference). The resulting communication-transportation overload may be especially burdensome for women, whose "workweeks," whatever the new tasks that fill it, remain long.

The leisure class today is not a class at all but a collection of occupational groups and age categories whose members (1) have motivation and opportunity to choose leisure over income or (2) are marginal to the economy and are therefore forced into leisure.

The former cross-cut class lines; they are part of a growing middle mass which draws from both above (college-educated engineers) and below (the upper-working class). Their motives for choosing leisure are shaped by the technical and social organization of work, and related leisure styles.

Marginal groups are concentrated in low-income, low-status jobs. The uneven distribution of non-work time among those working and the incidence of involuntary unemployment and retirement strongly suggest that men who have gained most leisure need and want more work. Here the "leisure stricken" are not replacing the "poverty stricken"; the two are becoming one.

Both major groups may stand in ever-sharper contrast to their more zealous colleagues at every level, and to the upper strata, who have what they have always had—the right to choose work as well as leisure.

NOTES

1. M. Kaplan, *Leisure in America: A Social Inquiry* (New York and London: John Wiley and Sons, 1960), p. 38.
2. The best of these is P. H. Douglas, *The Theory of Wages* (New York: Macmillan Co., 1934), pp. 295-314. Cf. T. A. Finegan, "Hours of Work in the United States: A Cross-sectional Analysis" (Unpublished Ph.D. dissertation, The University of Chicago, 1960), which ably and critically assesses, but in the main, confirms Douglas' findings, using better data—census week self-reports on "hours actually worked." The negative correlation between hours and earnings stands up well (−.69) in a multivariate analysis for occupations and in-

dustries characterized by large hours variance, but not so well else-where—e.g., in manufacturing.

3. H. L. Wilensky, "Work, Careers . . ." *op. cit.*

4. H. Webster, *Rest Days, A Study in Early Law and Morality* (New York: The Macmillan Co., 1916), p. 100. A recent expression is the Supreme Court's defense of blue laws as protection of secular rest.

5. *Ibid.*, p. 304.

6. J. Fourastié, *The Causes of Wealth* (translated and edited by T. Caplow; Glencoe, Illinois: The Free Press, 1960), pp. 171-73. A ten-month year in the upper civil service in Britain was usual in 1800 and prevailed until World War II. Since then, weekly hours increased from 38½ (6 days) to 42½ (5 days) and annual leave was cut back to a maximum of six weeks. That makes about 1,955 hours per year—close to the situation of antiquity but much more leisured than the American counterpart.

7. Fourastié, *op. cit.*, p. 164.

8. *Le livre des métiers d'Etienne Boileau,* XIIIᵉ Siecle, in the collection Les métiers et corporations de la ville de Paris (Paris: Imprimerie nationale, 1879), pp. 1-285 *passim.*

9. Émile Levasseur, *Histoire des classes ouvrières et de l'industrie en France avant 1789* (2nd ed.; Paris: Arthur Rousseau, 1901), I, 320-22, 328-29, 690.

10. Alfred Franklin, *La vie privée d'autrefois* (Paris: E. Plon, Nourrit et Cie, 1889), Vol. 5, pp. 125-216, 138.

11. Edouard Dolléans and Gérard Dehove, *Histoire du travail en France,* I (Paris: Domat-Montchrestien, 1953), 97-98.

12. Levasseur, *op. cit.,* II, 237, 385-88.

13. Fourastié, *op. cit.,* p. 38.

14. *Ibid.,* p. 91.

15. For the 1840's, Woytinsky estimates an 80-hour week for unspecified populations of "Continental Europe," Wladimir S. and E. S. Woytinsky, *World Population and Production* (Twentieth Century Fund, 1953), p. 366; and a 78-hour week for U.S.A. and France, W. S. Woytinsky, "Hours of Labor," *Encyclopaedia of the Social Sciences,* Vol. VII (New York: Macmillan Co., 1935), p. 479.

16. *Loc. cit.*

17. C. D. Long gives the most reliable estimate for the average labor force member. In each of the four countries offering usable data, the "standard" workweek (not adjusted for layoffs, strikes, sickness, turnover, etc.), weighted by the number of persons in the major industry categories (including agriculture, domestic service, and government), declined as follows:

Country	Dates	Decrease per decade in weekly hours of work
U. S. A.	1890-1950	4.2
Great Britain	1911-1951	3.3
Canada	1921-1941	3.5
Germany	1895-1950	3.2

The Labor Force under Changing Income and Employment (Princeton: Princeton University Press, 1958), pp. 140, 270-74.

18. U. S. Department of Commerce, *Statistical Abstract of the United States 1960*, pp. 224-26. Industry variations in rates of technological progress is a major factor. Recently brewing, baking, printing, and the ladies garment industry, all undergoing rapid technological change, have moved to standard workweeks shorter than 40. S. Brandwein, "Recent Accomplishments," in *The Shorter Work Week* (Washington, D. C.: Public Affairs Press, 1957), pp. 65-75.

19. Bogue, *op. cit.*, pp. 515-16.

20. For the larger study a factor analysis of the combined samples was done to clean up 34 measures of control variables such as "opportunity to stylize leisure" and "preoccupational leisure training." Length of vacation loads .42 on a high SES factor defined by high family income, occupation, and education.

21. Based on Stuart Garfinkle, "Changes in Working Life of Men, 1900-2000," *Monthly Labor Review*, 78 (March, 1955), Table 1, p. 299.

22. Jaffe and Carleton, *op. cit.*, p. 50. In keeping with a market definition of work, we make the wry assumption that the training period is "leisure."

23. H. L. Wilensky, "Life Cycle, Work Situation, and Participation in Formal Associations," Chapter 8 of R. W. Kleemeier, ed., *Aging and Leisure* (New York: Oxford University Press, 1961), pp. 227ff.

24. C. Long, *op. cit.*, p. 275.

25. Bogue, *op. cit.*, p. 463.

26. For further details, see H. L. Wilensky, "Orderly Careers and Social Participation: The Impact of Work History on Social Integration in the Middle Mass," *American Sociological*, 26 (August, 1961).

27. The factor analysis shows that working many hours a week is closely related to working many hours weekends, increasing hours in the past five years, and having control over one's own schedule. This factor appears to be unrelated to moonlighting (now and/or many years) or having a working wife (now or for a large part of married life.) Long weekly hours is only one of three independent

expressions of the choice of income over leisure. I will report data on the moonlighter elsewhere.

28. Does this contradict the economists' finding of a negative correlation between earnings and weekly hours? Two explanations for the discrepancies seem plausible: (1) Douglas and others deal with regressions of the means of earnings by occupation and industry on hours, a procedure by which our busy people may be lost to view—offset by the extremes on the other side of the mean; (2) the income and hours data in this study may be more complete (reliance on respondents' self-reports of all jobs, all days, not wives' reports, and of total annual family income, not weekly earnings of main earner).

29. See H. L. Wilensky, "Work, Careers . . .," *op. cit.*, which discusses the relation of these variables to leisure style; and "Orderly Careers . . .," *op. cit.*, which indicates that career type predicts social relations better than income, age, or occupational stratum.

30. Census data show that at every occupational level, the self-employed report longer hours than their salaried or wage-worker counterparts. E.g., in the census week of 1950, self-employed male "managers, officials, and proprietors, except farm" worked 56.1 hours on average—8.9 hours more than the mean wage-and-salary men in that classification. Finegan, *op. cit.*, pp. 41-42.

31. Emile Durkheim observed that "The divisions into days, weeks, months, years, etc. correspond to the periodical recurrence of rites, feasts, and public ceremonies. A calendar expresses the rhythm of collective activities, while at the same time its function is to assure their regularity." *The Elementary Forms of the Religious Life* (Glencoe, Illinois: The Free Press, 1947 [first published 1915]), pp. 10-11. Cf. P. A. Sorokin and R. K. Merton, "Social Time: A Methodological and Functional Analysis," *The American Journal of Sociology*, 42 (March, 1937), pp. 615-29.

32. Cf. R. J. Smith *et al.*, "Cultural Differences in the Life Cycle and the Concept of Time," in Kleemeier, *op. cit.*, pp. 83ff., and W. Moore, "The Exportability of the 'Labor Force' Concept," *American Sociological Review*, 18 (February, 1953), pp. 68-72. In several pre-literate societies, religious festivals and days thought unlucky or unsafe for work came to about half a year. Webster, *op. cit.*, pp. 303-4. If men are working only when they are gaining sustenance, then many "primitive" men had far more work-free time than we have. Cf. F. Cottrell. "The Sources of Free Time," in Kleemeier, *op. cit.*, p. 77.

33. Two excellent reviews of the evidence are: C. Long, *op. cit.*, and M. S. Gordon, *op. cit.* All facts and inferences on this point are from these sources unless otherwise specified. Long states that "No statistical evidence could be found . . . that the decline has been

the immediate result of increases in real income, extension of pensions and social security, physical deterioration (compared with elderly men in earlier periods), or of changes in self-employment, the pace of industry, or the level of employment," although older men have dropped out in periods of *very* high unemployment. Long, *op. cit.*, pp. 23, 13.

34. Bogue, *op. cit.*, p. 498ff.

35. Cf. Gordon, *op. cit.*, pp. 31ff.; and F. A. Pinner, P. Jacobs, and P. Selznick, *Old Age and Political Behavior* (Berkeley, California: University of California Press, 1959), pp. 65-67. There is also an increase in part-time unstable patterns of work among the aged. Gordon, *op. cit.*, p. 46. By 1956, one-fourth of male workers (65 and over) and more than 40 per cent of female workers of the same age were part-time employees (and their reasons were *non*-economic). Bouge, *op. cit.*, p. 450.

36. *Ibid.*, pp. 642, 644.

37. See the work of D. Riesman, e.g., Riesman and W. Bloomberg in C. Arensberg *et al.*, eds., *Research in Industrial Human Relations* (New York: Harper and Bros., 1957), p. 70. Cf. M. Mead, "The Pattern of Leisure in Contemporary American Culture," in E. Larrabee and R. Meyersohn, eds., *Mass Leisure* (Glencoe, Illinois: The Free Press, 1958), p. 15. For a contrasting interpretation, see H. L. Wilensky, "Work, Careers . . .," *op. cit.*

38. U. S. Bureau of Labor Statistics, *Composition of Payroll Hours in Manufacturing*, Bulletin 1283 (October, 1960), p. 1. Vacations accounted for 3.6 per cent; holidays, 2.2 per cent; sick leave and all other leave, less than 0.3 per cent. Since the survey period was a time of slack, the ratio of leave to hours paid for may be above normal. About three in five of these workers received one to two weeks' vacation; fewer than 3 per cent were paid for more than three weeks.

39. H. G. Lewis estimates that the fraction of the increased leisure per head since 1900 taken in the form of rest periods, coffee breaks, and the like is no larger than five per cent. "Hours of Work and Hours of Leisure," *Ninth Annual Proceedings,* Industrial Relations Research Association (publication #18), December 28 and 29, 1956, p. 205.

40. B. Karsh, "The Meaning of Work in an Age of Automation," *Current Economic Comment,* 19 (August, 1957), pp. 10-11. Cf. W. A. Faunce "Automation in the Automobile Industry: Some Consequences for In-plant Social Structure," *American Sociological Review,* 23 (August, 1958), pp. 401-7. J. Stieber, "Automation and the White-Collar Worker," *Personnel* 34 (November-December 1957), pp. 8-17. An offsetting factor in fully-automated plants is the increase in sophisticated maintenance jobs. Some of these jobs require that

men patrol the plant alone on a fixed round, but many permit freer sociability.

41. A. Heckscher, and S. de Grazia, "Problems in Review: Executive Leisure," *Harvard Business Review,* 37 (July-August, 1959), p. 10. Table based on a 30 per cent mail return from a sample of 17,000 executives—a random selection of 12,000 from *Harvard Business Review* subscribers plus 5,000 names from *Poor's Register of Directors and Executives.*

42. R. Sheehan, "The Executive Lunch," *Fortune,* 57 (January, 1958), pp. 120-21. This is not to say that elites do not continue to mix business and pleasure, only that the number of undiluted business hours is large.

43. J. A. Krout, *Annals of American Sport (Vol. 15 of Pageant of America;* New Haven: Yale University Press, 1929), p. 2.

44. H. Chafetz, *Play the Devil: A History of Gambling in the United States from 1492-1955* (New York: Clarkson N. Potter, 1960), p. 31.

45. F. R. Dulles, *America Learns to Play* (New York: D. Appleton-Century Co., 1940), pp. 88ff., 90-91.

46. N. J. Smelser, *Social Change in the Industrial Revolution* (Chicago: The University of Chicago Press, 1959), pp. 193, 183, 298ff.

47. H. L. Wilensky and C. N. Lebeaux, *Industrial Society and Social Welfare* (New York: Russell Sage Foundation, 1958), pp. 56ff. While we "spend" time, "save" time, and "waste" it, modern Greek villagers, like many other contemporary peasants and primitives, "pass" the time. M. Mead, ed., *Cultural Patterns and Technical Change* (New York: New American Library, Mentor Book, 1955), pp. 70-72. Simmel, of course, chose the clock as a symbol of modern life, in which so much rests on a time-cost calculation. ". . . The technique of metropolitan life is unimaginable without the most punctual integration of all activities and mutual relations into a stable and impersonal time schedule." "The Metropolis and Mental Life" in *The Sociology of Georg Simmel* (translated by K. W. Wolf; Glencoe, Illinois: The Free Press, 1950), p. 413.

48. H. L. Wilensky, "Work, Careers . . .," *op. cit.,* pp. 543-60.

49. We are all familiar with the dentist or doctor who "freely" imposes on himself an impossible patient load. Recently, however, more physicians have entered group practice, with cooperative hospital rounds, shorter office hours, telephone-answering services and direct connection among partners' homes, plus a cut-back on house calls. These changes permit a "family day" off and longer out-of-town vacations. A more general response is to allocate to less-trained persons tasks formerly performed by the men in short supply; we see this in medicine, dentistry, teaching, social work,

engineering and science. Finally, increased productivity via further mechanization can permit a cut-back in hours—and it is true that occupations marked by technological progress have gained more leisure than those established service and professional occupations marked by traditional work habits. In the short run, however, these trends are unlikely to offset the increased demand for scarce talent and the resulting climb in the price of leisure.

50. See e.g., G. Brooks, "Historical Background," in *The Shorter Work Week* (Washington, D. C.: Public Affairs Press, 1957), pp. 7-19.

51. The latter takes more workers for equivalent output, decreases flexibility in production planning, and increases labor costs. In seasonal peaks (tomato season for food canning, Lent for the Boston fish market, new model runs for the auto industry), the enterprise must pay overtime, or bear standby and substitute costs. If extra shifts are necessary, changeover time is increased. Vacation and holiday schedules, in contrast, can be staggered, predictably and cheaply (production falls off anyway around Christmas and in the summer), or the workplace can be shut down for repairs, re-tooling, and the like. There are exceptions. Under union pressure, the rubber companies adopted six 6-hour days in the 1930's—partly as a work-sharing device. Goodyear President Litchfield later said that efficiency went up under this schedule. It is possible, however, that the coercive effect of the depression and an accelerated incentive pace account for the increases, not the six-hour day. By 1957, only about one in seven rubber workers was on this unusual schedule. W. L. Ginsburg and R. Bergmann, "The Workers' Viewpoint" in *Ibid.*, pp. 35-37.

52. A Soviet writer said that in 1960 there would be a return to the seven-hour day, six-day week that prevailed before World War II. He predicts that in 1964 the working day will be five or six hours (six days), or six or seven hours (five days), depending upon the nature of the work. There is an assumption in such writings that increased leisure should come in the form of a shorter workday. The rationale: to "reduce the extreme intensification of labor" (attributed to "capitalism") and permit more investment of daily time in study and training. N. P. Kostin, "Free Time Under Communism," *The Soviet Review*, I (August, 1960), 28ff. Cf. Alec Nove (University of London), "The State and the Wage Earner," *Soviet Survey*, No. 26 (October-December, 1958), p. 31; and D. Allchurch, "Diversions and Distractions," *Soviet Survey*, No. 26 (October-December, 1958), p. 49.

53. Allchurch, *ibid.*, p. 49.

54. Kostin, *op. cit.*, p. 31.

55. L. N. Kogan, "The Nature of Work in the Future Communist Society," *The Soviet Review*, I (August, 1960), 23.

56. "In 1958, upwards of 2,500 workers in the Sverdlovsk economic area were enlisted to act as vocational training instructors. Kogan, *op. cit.*, p. 21.

57. A survey of 11 major urban labor markets reports that 12 to 31 per cent of workers in manufacturing were on shift work in the winter of 1958-59. U. S. Department of Labor, *Wages and Related Benefits, 20 Labor Markets, 1958-59*, Bureau of Labor Statistics, Bulletin No. 1240-22 (November, 1959), p. 5.

58. F. C. Mann and L. R. Hoffman, *Automation and the Worker: A Study of Social Change in Power Plants* (New York: Henry Holt & Co., 1960), p. 112ff.

59. A comparison of rotating shift workers with day workers in one oil refinery suggests that the shift workers' activities were a function of their flexibility: these workers spent more leisure time gardening, working around the house and yard, fixing things—activities that can be done almost anytime. Careful examination of the tables reported, however, shows no significant restriction of formal and informal social contacts. E. Blakelock, "A New Look at the New Leisure," *Administrative Science Quarterly*, 4 (March, 1960), pp. 446-67.

60. In the U. S., women workers are concentrated in jobs which involve (1) traditional housewives' tasks—cooking, cleaning, sewing, and canning; (2) few or no strenuous physical activities and hazards; (3) patience, waiting, routine; (4) rapid use of hands and fingers such as office machine operating and electrical assembling; (5) a distinctive welfare or cultural orientation; (6) contact with young children; and (7) sex appeal. Bogue, *op. cit.*, pp. 491-92. In developing countries, where the mass media and other industrial influences whet the appetite for consumer goods, women may be even more eager to work. A study of three areas of the Puerto Rican labor market shows that a majority of the adult female population have been drawn into the labor force and about nine in ten of the women workers interviewed, married or single, want to work indefinitely. P. Gregory, "The Labor Market in Puerto Rico," in W. E. Moore and A. S. Feldman, *Labor Commitment and Social Change in Developing Areas* (New York: Social Science Research Council, 1960), pp. 136-72. In more advanced economics it is possible that automation will wipe out many clerical and semi-skilled manual jobs now held by women—that both office and factory will be put more in the hands of men. R. Dubin, *The World of Work* (New York: Prentice-Hall, 1958), p. 202. Whether the rising demand for females in service and professional occupations will offset this development depends upon the rate of economic growth, the age composition of the population (labor shortages), enterprise tolerance of turnover, etc.

61. K. W. Deutsch lists some reasons: rising labor costs, fixed

budgets, the rising costs of able managers for small or middle-sized establishments, the difficulty of dividing units of managerial effort to man the extra hours. "On Social Communication and the Metropolis," *Daedalus*, 90 (Winter, 1961), p. 105. The capital investment for serving a horde of people at rush hours is, of course, vastly greater than that required if they staggered their leisure.

JOEL E. GERSTL

University College of
South Wales & Monmouthshire
(Cardiff)

8

Leisure, Taste and Occupational Milieu*

"Leisure—even for those who do not work—is at bottom a function of work, flows from work, and changes as the nature of work changes."[1]

While the question of the fusion and/or polarity of work and leisure has frequently been considered, the referent has usually been a generic one. Most often, the focus has been upon the situation of the industrial worker, or upon contrasts between the masses and the classes, or between society-wide status levels.[2] Certainly, in considering leisure as a social problem—for example, in projecting the differential changes in the workweek to a future in which the bulk of the population will work shorter hours while managerial and professional strata will continue to carry work home evenings and weekends—analysis must remain concerned with wide societal categories. However, to contrast manual workers' patterns of leisure with those of professional people is not to explain the differences. It may well be that much of the explanation of social class differences in the uses of leisure is spurious to the extent that such research obfuscates

* Reprinted from *Social Problems*, Vol. 9, No. 1, Summer, 1961. A revised version of a paper read at the meetings of the Society for the Study of Social Problems, New York, August, 1960.

contrasts *within* a stratum. Whether spurious or not, this type of analysis fails to reveal the crucial link between structure and behavior.

It is not merely *because* a person is high in the prestige hierarchy of his society that he takes work home or belongs to a chamber music society (although he may well do both in order to maintain or reinforce his high status). While prestigeful leisure behavior is of course related to social class position, its explanation must be linked to intervening variables.

It is the argument of this paper that incumbency in a particular occupational milieu is one of the most crucial of these intervening variables. For, while the existence of occupational milieus is a seemingly patent feature of life, and while the descriptive literature of occupational sociology is voluminous, the importance of occupation upon style of life in studies of stratification has been minimized by using occupation merely as an index (or part of an index) of social placement.

In order to examine the effect of membership in a particular occupation upon non-occupational behavior while holding social class constant, it is obviously necessary to contrast occupations at approximately the same prestige level whose work situation differs considerably. Three upper-middle class occupational situations have been chosen for this purpose: the independent professional practitioner, the organization man of the corporate world, and the salaried intellectual. The occupations representing these three types are: the dentist (one of the few professionals still predominantly in solo practice and strangely enough almost missing from the growing sociological literature on professions), the adman (an intriguing villain of contemporary social criticism and archetype of the organizational world), and the college professor (an anomaly in the social order with high prestige and an incommensurate income).

The present study is based upon interviews, using both structured and open-ended items, with 75 respondents, one-third in each of the occupational groups, all conducted by the writer. The dentists and admen were from a large Midwestern city in the United States; the college professors were on the faculty of a small residential college, which will be referred to as Sauk College, located some distance from an urban center. As a result of pre-determined controls for occupational stability and stage in life cycle, all respondents were around the age of forty.[3]

The aim of this study is exploratory: to examine the links between occupational milieu—including the nature of the work performed, the setting of the work situation, and the norms derived from occupational reference groups—and non-occupational behavior, the realm of leisure. The examination of leisure is undertaken in terms of its range—from the narrow circle of family, outward to the larger community.[4]

Home Life

There is probably no major activity under the broad heading of leisure which is more difficult to account for accurately than is time which is spent "at home." Without having attempted a detailed time-budget, the following account is restricted to the most salient categories revealed in response to open-ended questions concerning the ways evenings and weekends were spent. These categories were: time with children, household chores, television viewing, reading, work-connected activities and specific recreational interests.

A major occupational contrast is the extent to which working time permeates the rest of life. This is clearly the basic effect of the structure of the work situation and of the possibilities stemming from the nature of particular types of work. The professors' 56-60 hour work-week necessarily includes evening and weekend work, usually done at home. The admen's working schedule averages 45 hours a week; although crises and deadlines seem ever-present, few do night work more than a dozen times a month. It comes as no great surprise that the dentists do not take their work home; their 40 hours a week rarely spill-over beyond office time.[5]

Interestingly, the nature of occupational milieu explains not only the actual distribution of working time, but also orientation to hypothetical time. The striking differences between occupations are shown in Table 1. In considering what they might do with two extra hours in the day, professors expressed no desire

TABLE 1

Hypothetical Use of Two Extra Hours by Occupation

Activity	Admen	Dentists	Professors
Relaxation	12.1%	29.4%	0.0%
Family-home	24.3	14.7	9.4
Recreational reading	12.1	14.7	28.1
Hobby or recreation	33.3	32.4	12.5
Work or work-connected reading	18.2	8.8	50.0
Total	100%	100%	100%
Number of responses°	(33)	(34)	(32)

° Multiple responses were given.

to relax and are most inclined to work more. The dentists wanted above all to spend time with their hobbies and recreational activities; almost an equal number gave first priority to relaxation, as they are tired after a long day of standing on their feet. Admen are equally desirous of recreational time, with family and home activity their second alternative. These contrasting wishes suggest that it is not merely high occupational prestige which makes for the convergence of work and leisure as previous research has indicated.[6]

While the amount of time spent with one's children is difficult to estimate accurately, respondents' statements can be readily rated as great, moderate or minimal. (Minimal time would, in the extreme, involve being with children only at meals.) The admen and dentists do not differ greatly in the amount of time spent with their children; 40 per cent of the former and 30 per cent of the latter spend a minimal amount of time in this activity, in sharp contrast, two-thirds of the professors do.[7]

The modal estimate of time devoted to household chores is between three and seven hours for each of the three groups. But, one-third of the professors, one-fifth of the admen and only a single dentist do *no* household work. This almost universal activity in household tasks among dentists is likely to be an indication of work upon leisure—in his facility in tinkering and the use of his hands.

Both dentists and admen watch television for a modal five to ten hours, with one-third in each group watching 11 to 20 hours. Their viewing habits are considerably below the national average of 18 hours a week,[8] albeit interviewing was done in the spring, when a man's fancy turns from the tube. The situation among the professors is quite different, for extended TV viewing is strongly against the norms of Sauk. Indeed, over half of the professors do not own a television set, and are proud of it. Two-thirds of the owners claim to watch less than four hours a week, and all but one of the rest watch less than ten hours. The one exception was quite conscious of his deviancy from Sauk TV norms.

The home life of the Sauk professor is distinct from that of the other groups largely due to the pervasiveness of his work-connected activities. Much of the time that the adman and the dentist spends with his children or watching TV is, for the professor, spent in his work. Probably this allows him to get away with doing less around the house.[9] The adman spends somewhat less time in household chores and with his children than does the dentist. The working hours and schedules of each as well as alternative recreational interests and amounts of time devoted to reading (which will be considered subsequently) help to account for these contrasting patterns.

Recreation and Vacation

Most obvious from the information conveyed in Table 2 is the sedentary way of life of the Sauk professors—not only in their work, but in their leisure as well.[10] Forty per cent took part in no sports activity of any kind; for all but three of the others, the extent of participation was low. While admen and dentists are represented in approximately an equal number of sports, the admen are more active. For example, the number of admen and dentists playing golf is almost identical, but while most of the dentists play but once a week, the admen play twice a week or more. Partially this is a result of the respective work schedules—the adman has more of a chance to sneak in nine holes or more during a "working" day. More important for the adman is the fairly common conduct of business on the green

TABLE 2

Index of Sports Activity by Occupation°

Activity	Admen	Dentists	Professors
Golf	32	27	0
Hunting	7	18	1
Fishing	17	28	5
Bowling	8	4	0
Swimming	29	13	10
Boating-Sailing	8	2	2
Hiking-Walking	13	1	10
Skiing	10	0	3
Tennis	9	6	6
Other activities	18	19	10
Total recreational score	151	118	47

° The index consists of a combination of the number of respondents mentioning an activity (in response to the question: Do you take part in any recreational activities?) times the frequency of participation score. Infrequent = 1, Moderate = 2, Heavy = 3.

or in the club. Indeed, some indicated that they must play golf for business reasons, even though they do not like the game.

Another function of physical recreation frequently volunteered by the admen is for the release of strain and tension, which they admit to be considerable. While the dentist also feels great strains in his work—many are surprisingly sensitive about their sadistic functional role—the nature of work strains are quite different in the two cases. Both view physical recreation as escape, but for one it is to "blow off steam," for the other it is mainly to relax. While the adman finds his satisfactions in frequent and active sports, the dentist indulges more in routinized golf and seasonal hunting and fishing.

Items mentioned by respondents as hobbies include activities pursued frequently and with great zeal as well as sporadic or habitual time fillers. In spite of this ambiguity, there are occupational contrasts.

The most frequent hobby, mentioned by more than half of the dentists, consists of some variety of "do-it-yourself"—ranging from home repairs to wood-working to gardening. Only in one case was there a more immediate and direct vocational link to avocational interests, represented by metallurgical research.

Vocational influences are stronger among the admen. Reading and painting received almost as many mentions as did the do-it-yourself category. Half of those who paint in their leisure had in mind the non-commercial counterpart of their vocation; for the others, the day-to-day interaction with artists is probably a motivating factor. Similarly, references to writing were also frequent, involving the transfer of verbal facility from the writing of copy to the writing of "the great American novel" (or short stories for *Playboy*).

The professors care least for do-it-yourself. Music is the most frequent recreational activity at Sauk. Two-thirds of the professors mentioned it as a major leisure interest, and half of these are active participants in instrumental and vocal groups. In addition to general reading, many professors expressed interest in disciplines related to their own fields. In some cases this was thought of as the inseparable nature of literature, music, and art. In others, it was more a matter of the desire for intellectual awareness as such—the humanist might even read *The Organization Man* before blasting the sociologist.

Differences in vacation patterns clearly reveal occupational structuring. The adman's modal two or three weeks is a function of corporation policy. Less than a third of the professors take the full academic summer, but the potential is there—subject, above all, to financial possibility. Curiously, dentists have the most clearly defined vacation norm—three weeks—even though theirs is the most autonomous decision.

The fusion of work into leisure is again greatest among the professors. Even those who take the entire academic vacation claim not to forsake their calling, whether in European travel or a summer cottage in Maine. The majority of the professors, however, do not remain unemployed for the entire summer. Since Sauk has no summer school, they either teach elsewhere, take part in research projects, or hold positions in industry.

Almost half of the Sauk professors also take trips away from campus during Christmas vacation or between semesters; these are frequently a combination of attendance at professional meetings and other purposes. Most of the dentists, on the other hand, do not attend professional meetings outside the state. Business trips are quite frequent for the admen, one-fifth spending a week or more each month in travel. Of course not all of this time is spent entirely in work.

Visiting and Viewing

Although the admen are slightly more gregarious than the other two occupational groups, differences are minor. Four-fifths of the admen and three-fourths of the dentists and professors visit with friends at least once a week; more admen than either of the other groups visit more than once a week. The dentists have a larger number of close friends than do the admen or professors—the median number for them is six, while it is five for the latter two occupations.[11]

The content and purpose of social relations with friends varies among the three groups. Perhaps the major distinction centers upon patterns of conversation-drinking by admen, cardplaying by dentists, and conversation-eating by the Sauk professors. The frequent exchange of dinners in the last mentioned group reflects the social life of a small community. Although the cardplaying evenings of the dentists are sometimes accompanied by dinners, commensalism is less frequent for them than it is among the professors and is least frequent among admen. The emphasis upon conversation on the part of the admen and professors, as contrasted with the cardplaying dentists, might well be a reflection of occupationally based verbal facility. Obviously, this is not to suggest that the dentists do not talk to their friends, but it would appear that while small talk during cardplaying is not thought of as a social *activity*, conversation—whether about people, ideas or business (not about teeth)—is more likely to be considered an end in itself.

While all three occupational groups visit with friends more frequently than is usual for an urban cross-section, admen and dentists visit with relatives at a rate roughly comparable to the population as a whole.[12] The majority of admen and dentists see their relatives (and/or in-laws), at least once a week, one-fifth of each group see them twice a month, and the rest only several times a year or less. The Sauk professors, on the other hand, typically live far away from relatives and tend to see them but annually.

Apart from family life, recreational activity, and visiting, a consideration of uses of leisure time must also include spectator activities (supplementary to the previously discussed television viewing). Most relevant are attendance at movies and sports events.[13]

The Sauk professors attend movies more frequently than do either of the other two groups. Three-fourths attend at least once a month, and half at least twice a month. Certainly this is connected with their limited exposure to television. By sharp contrast, 44 per cent of the admen and only 28 per cent of the dentists attend once a month or more. One-fourth of the admen and almost half of the dentists hardly ever go to the movies; this is true of only three of the professors. While the contrast between admen and dentists is not great, the latter attend movies less frequently.

There are only minor occupational differences in attendance at sports events. One-fourth of the admen, over one-third of the dentists, and one-fifth of the professors never attend.[14] In each case, the modal pattern is to attend between five and ten games in the course of the year. The enthusiasts, those who attend eleven games or more, do not include more than a fifth of any of the groups.

Voluntary Associations

While membership in occupational associations is to a large extent dictated by particular occupational roles, the amount of participation represents an area of activity which falls between the spheres of work and leisure. The dentists are most active in their professional societies, while the Sauk professors are significantly less active than either of the other two groups. The consideration of participation in organizations which are not directly connected with the work role of the respondents again reveals the academic group to be least active.

Almost half of the Sauk professors denied even nominal membership in any non-professional organization. Negative responses included references to the "absurd waste of time that such nonsense often results in," and the virtue of a small town that does not necessitate such activity. One-fifth mentioned membership in a church or with a church-connected group as their only organizational affiliation. One-fourth were involved in college activities—including athletic, musical and social groups. In addition there were scattered references to membership in PTA, and activity with scout groups. There were but two major deviations from the norm of low participation and minimal activity in the non-college community.

The dentists belong to a larger number of groups than the admen, but participate less in each. Hence in an index which combines the number of organizations with a measure of the extent of participation, admen and dentists are quite similar. The high association between participation in occupational and other types of voluntary organizations for all three groups is shown in Table 3. This relationship—indicating that participation in professional societies is part of the syndrome of "joiner"—is strongest for the admen and the professors. Admen tend to be active in both professional and non-professional groups, professors in neither. The majority of dentists are active in their professional associations, whether or not they are active in other groups.

Unlike the Sauk professors, most admen and dentists are at

TABLE 3

Extent of Participation in Voluntary Associations by Extent of Participation in Occupational Associations

Voluntary Associations	Professional Associations	
	Low	High
Low	77%	35%
High	23	65
Total	100%	100%
Number of cases	(35)	(40)

Chi square = 13.8, $p < .001$.

least moderately active in various associations. While one-third of the professors hold no formal organizational memberships —outside of their professional societies—only one dentist and two admen are in a similar position.

The type of organization in which membership is held, as indicated in Table 4, is even more revealing of occupational differences than is the designation of the extent of participation. The most striking contrast is the concentration of dentists in fraternal organizations and that of admen in civic activity.

While it is not necessary to posit the furthering of one's contracts for "business" reasons as the sole justification for membership in fraternal organizations, and while there probably is a segregation of work interests and leisure fellowship for some, business reasons are probably an important determinant of the large number of memberships by dentists in these groups. Similar reasons might also be relevant to their other memberships.

The dentists are not only the most active in church organizations, but are also most regular—or most compulsive—in attendance. All but two of the Protestant[15] dentists attend church at least three times a month, half claiming regular weekly attendance. By contrast, one-third of the Protestant admen and almost half of the professors attend church but several times a year, or not at all. One-fourth of the professors and a slightly larger proportion of the admen attend weekly.

TABLE 4

Types of Organizational Membership for Admen and Dentists

Type of Organization	Admen	Dentists
Church committees and clubs	4	12
Fraternal	3	24
Youth service	10	9
Civic	24	9
Recreational	19	12
Total number of organizational memberships	60*	66*

* Includes multiple memberships.

The extremes represented by the dentists and the professors are highlighted in that in the course of answering questions concerning religious attendance, the dentists apologized for not attending more, the professors for attending as much as they did.

Whatever the specific motivations for the differential membership and participation patterns, these patterns are indicators of life style. For the dentists, the concentration is in fraternal and church groups. This range of participation would in part explain the social image which they hold of themselves. For, although they consider their occupational prestige to be high, they insist that their social position is not more than middle-class.[16]

In light of the positions held by many of the admen in large agencies, it would be less likely that membership in any voluntary association would be of direct assistance to them in terms of business contacts. Their occupational role does, however, explain the heavy concentration in civic work. About half of the admen have done work with voluntary health organizations and/or the Community Chest. Frequently this activity is part of their occupational role, utilizing vocational skills—for example, they may be the representative of their firm for a particular drive, or do the art work in a campaign. Often the activity may begin as part of their work task and then continue beyond it—in terms of both time and involvement. A more direct vocational link exists when a client is interested in a voluntary organization. But the range of civic activities is considerably wider than that which is represented by policy dictates of firms or clients.[17]

Just as the profession as a whole attempts to raise its societal image by concerted public service efforts through the Advertising Council of America, so local occupational associations and particular companies attempt to foster this type of activity. The larger companies all heartily support the time and effort their employees put into public service campaigns. Indeed, they advertise this activity. The occupation's attempt at raising its image has a counterpart on the level of the individuals involved. In spite of the admen's enthusiastic statements of devotion to his work, he is bothered by the low status of his calling. He hopes that by doing good works he can help to alleviate the nasty image which, in spite of his protests, clings in the mind of the public. Certainly the striving for higher occupational prestige would be a major factor in determining the type of activity to which time and effort is devoted. While the adman recognizes the low status of his work he accords himself a high standing in his community.[18] His activity in civic associations helps to fill this gap.

The spread of various types of leisure time activities throughout the societal strata of the contemporary United States does not make it possible to ascribe prestige to *types* of recreational clubs. However, on the basis of an intuitive ranking of the prestige of the *particular* clubs in which respondents hold membership, it would appear that the admen more than the dentists belong to groups of a higher prestige level.

Consideration of the participation patterns of the respondents' wives in voluntary associations affords further indication of the contrasts in the life styles of the three groups. Each manifests a unique pattern as Table 5 indicates.

The correspondence of prestige levels of the organizational participation of husbands and wives is striking. Dentists reveal a life style consonant with a middle-class image, with fraternal lodges for the husbands and church clubs for the wives. The

TABLE 5

Wives' Organizational Participation by Occupation of Husband

Range of Participation	Admen	Dentists	Professors
None	42%	33%	23%
Church groups only	8	21	4
Local groups*	17	46	55
Civic, charity and professional	33	0	18
Total	100%	100%	100%
Number of wives	(24)	(24)	(22)

* The category designated as local groups consists of neighborhood women's clubs, youth service groups such as Boy Scouts, and the Parent-Teacher's Association. Women's auxiliary groups of their husband's occupations have also been included in this middle category.

upper-middle class admen and their wives are, on the other hand, involved in a wider and more prestigeful range of organization—in the wider community.[19] Opportunities for organizational participation for the wives of the college professors are circumscribed. Indeed, the limitations of the community in this (as well as other) respects was a great source of discontent among faculty wives. Nevertheless, the academic wives, more than the wives of admen and dentists, do participate in at least some voluntary associations.

Taste

Apart from the general notion of range and of prestige levels, the foregoing analysis has been essentially quantitative: who does how much of what. A basic adjunct is in the realm of taste: who indulges in the "higher" things of life?

While the members of the three occupational groups are all more or less middlebrow (with a few possible shadings into high and low brow) in Lynes' use of the term,[20] the contrast between the extremes *within* the middlebrow category is most revealing. Accordingly, the present attempt is simply to make the gross distinction between "upper" and "lower" brow. Six items constitute the measure and operational definition of taste: attendance at theaters and concerts, musical taste, hours spent reading, number of books read, and types of magazines read.[21] The findings are summarized in Table 6.

The first two measures, of theater and concert going, indicate those who attended at least one performance in the past year. Although the Sauk professor must travel a considerable distance to attend non-college performances, he attended the theater twice as much as did the adman (the frequent business trips of the latter to Chicago and New York notwithstanding). The professors also attended the largest number of concert performances.

Upper-brow musical taste indicates a preference for classical music. The majority of dentists and admen favored "pops" or "quiet dance music." Two respondents, both dentists prefer "top-ten" tunes. One-fourth of the admen like "good jazz" in addition, or instead of, their diet of "pops." None of the dentists

TABLE 6

Percentage of Upperbrow Responses by Occupation

Brow Measures	Admen	Dentists	Professors
Theater attendance	68	32	64 (96)*
Concert attendance	44	28	64 (100)*
Musical taste	16	24	96
Hours reading	52	20	60†
Number of books	56	16	80†
Magazine type	0	0	68
Total score	236	120	432 (500)
Mean score	40	20	72 (83)

* The figures in parentheses include those who attended concerts and theaters only at Sauk.

† These figures refer to reading which is not concerned with work, a distinction many found difficult to make.

shared this taste. Most of the professors were more specific than "classical music" and several liked jazz in addition to the classics. Only one professor admitted preferring "light music" to classical. The pervasiveness of norms of musical taste at Sauk is corroborated by the high rate of attendance at Sauk concerts and in the amount of participation in musical groups by the faculty.

Comparison of taste and concert attendance reveals an interesting discrepancy. While only 16 per cent of the admen admit to enjoying classical music, 44 per cent have attended concerts in the past year. The implication is that 28 per cent of the admen doze through the concerts to which their wives drag them. The dentists are less concerned with this symbol of display —the discrepancy between likes and attendance consists of but a single person.

The dichotomy of high and low recreational reading was made on the basis of less than five hours and five or more. Although it is undoubtedly difficult to estimate the amount of time one has spent reading, less than five hours a week cannot involve very much more than the daily newspaper and glancing at some magazines.

Number of books read separates those who read at least one

(non-work connected) book in the last month and those who read less than ten in the last year. Detailed contrasts are sharper than the dichotomy reveals. Fifty-six per cent of the dentists had read *no* books in the last year, while one-fourth of the admen and three professors made similar admissions. At the other extreme, 44 per cent of the professors, one-fourth of the admen, and two dentists claimed to have read three or more books in the month preceding the interview.

The final measure distinguishes between higher and lower brow magazines. Lowerbrow subsumes most of the mass periodicals: *House and Garden, Life, Saturday Evening Post, Reader's Digest, Argosy*, and downward. The upper-brow category includes: *Harper's, The New Yorker, Saturday Review, Encounter*, and up through the little magazines.[22] The list of magazines read by each respondent was categorized according to direction of emphasis. Interestingly, there was almost no contamination—the reader of some higher-brow magazines reads many, and vice versa.

While it is no doubt rather disconcerting to find almost a third of the professors limiting themselves to lower-brow magazines, the zeros in Table 6 are no less than astounding. Apart from the cross-brow *Time* or *Newsweek*, the highest that the magazine brows of the dentists extend is to include a *New Yorker* and an *Esquire* thrown into a lower-brow diet. And the admen, the professional purveyors of the mass media, have brows extending no higher than an isolated reference to *Holiday* and *The American Heritage*.

Conclusion

While the effect of occupational role upon the rest of life is frequently proclaimed in the context of occupational sociology, it has seldom been examined in a comparative structural context. The foregoing comparison of admen, dentists and professors has attempted to reveal some of the links between occupational milieu and non-occupational behavior. The contrasts between occupations all in a similar social stratum indicate that the crucial explanatory factor is that of the occupational milieu—consisting of the setting of the work situation, the nature of the work performed, and the norms derived from occupational reference groups—which allows, dictates or is conducive to particular patterns of behavior.

The consequences of the structure of the work situation are seen most directly in the extent to which hours of work provide the framework for other activities. For example, the professor's long hours of academic involvement necessitate less time for his leisure and his home life. Alternatively, the fluidity of the adman's business routine may allow for recreational activity during the working day, a luxury in which the dentist is most unlikely to indulge himself. Certainly, contrasting vacation patterns are a function of working routine.

The nature of the work task has a variety of effects, the most immediate of which is dramatically illustrated in considering the possibility of the fusion of work with leisure. It is physically most difficult for the dentist to "take his work home" (although he could take X-rays home for study or return to his office to do laboratory work). But, even if the dentist does work overtime, this task is readily defined as *work*. The professor, by contrast, is likely to find it difficult to say whether reading in or around his field is working or not. Similarly, it is absurd even to think of the dentist bringing his work on his vacation; such a fusion is more likely for the adman, and becomes probable for the professor. The nature of these occupations involves different types of cultural demarcation and evaluation, one indication of which is seen in the responses of the three groups to the question of a hypothetical two hours (Table 1). Again, the professors are most likely to say they would do more work, the dentists least likely, and the admen to have an intermediary position on the subject.

Intrinsic in the nature of work is a specialization of skills. The extent to which such skills spill over into the realm of leisure is seen in contrasting hobby interests: use of their hands for the dentists, painting and writing for the admen, and intellectual pursuits for the professors. On the other hand, the nature of work in the context of particular work situations results in different types of strains, whether physical or emotional. These too are reflected in patterns of leisure, in "blowing off steam" for the admen and "taking things easy" for the dentists.

Participation in voluntary organizations may begin as a work task for the admen. But its justification (by either the admen or their organizations) is not only a function of their occupational skill, but also a rationalization and compensation for the marginal social status of their work. The types of organizational memberships in which the dentists are found also show both a direct occupational function—building a clientele—and a consequent status repercussion (Tables 4 and 5).

The influence of occupational reference groups appears to be most pervasive among the professors, as indicated by such norms as those against extended TV viewing or their similarities in musical taste, musical interest, and their high rates of attendance 'at theaters and concerts. Reference group influences are operative in the other groups also. Thus, it is not only the adman on the art side of the firm who paints for a hobby, but it is likely to be his influence which interests the account executive in a similar pursuit. Likewise, conviviality as a way of life, as evidenced by the admen's frequent cocktail parties, represents an occupational norm sanctioned by the reference group.

Although the account presented in this paper has emphasized the explanatory links between occupational factors and other types of behavior, one must be cautious of the tendency toward occupational determinism. Certainly such factors as national fads and fashions are most important in the analysis of leisure.[23] But even if do-it-yourself or painting seem to be sweeping the country at one particular period of time, the concentration of involvement with such activity in particular portions of the population still needs to be explained. The consideration of occupational milieu is crucial for this purpose, for it involves an individual's major connection with the larger social structure of which he is a part through the division of labor.

NOTES

1. Clement Greenberg, "Work and Leisure Under Industrialism," in *Mass Leisure* (Eric Larrabee and Rolf Meyersohn, eds.; Glencoe: The Free Press, 1958), p. 38.

2. The most immediate reference is David Riesman and Warner Bloomberg, Jr., "Work and Leisure: Fusion and Polarity?" in *Research in Industrial Human Relations* (Conrad M. Arensberg, et. al., eds.; New York: Harper and Brothers, 1957), and David Riesman, "Leisure and Work in Post-Industrial Society," in *Mass Leisure, op. cit.* Similar general referents are used in most of the literature in both the study of leisure and stratification; for example, Alfred C. Clarke, "The Use of Leisure and its Relations to Levels of Occupational Prestige," *American Sociological Review*, 21 (June, 1956), pp. 301-7; Leonard Reissman, "Social Class, Leisure and Social Participation," *American Sociological Review*, 19 (February, 1954), pp. 76-84; R. Clyde White, "Social Class Differences in the Use of Leisure," *American Journal of Sociology*, LXI (September, 1955), 145-50.

3. For a detailed discussion of sample selection and sample characteristics, see Joel E. Gerstl, *Career Commitment and Style of Life in Three Middle Class Occupations* (Unpublished doctoral dissertation, University of Minnesota, 1959), pp. 27-50.

4. This model is similar to that employed in the Kansas City Study of Adult Life. See Robert J. Havighurst, "The Leisure Activities of the Middle-Aged," *American Journal of Sociology*, LXIII (September, 1957), 152-62, and Robert J. Havighurst and Kenneth Feigenbaum, "Leisure and Life Style," *American Journal of Sociology*, LXIV (January, 1959), 396-404.

5. Working hours were ascertained by asking for a detailed account of the respondents' daily routine, with probes for evening and week-end work.

6. Alfred C. Clarke, *op. cit.*, used the identical question of a hypothetical two hours. He finds the desire to work, read, or study to increase as one goes up in prestige level; those lowest on his prestige scale want, above all, to relax, loaf, and sleep. Curiously, he reports no category of hobbies or recreation.

7. The use of the hypothetical two hours (Table 1) is relevant here. It suggests that the admen *want* most to spend more time with their children, feeling that they do not spend sufficient time at present, and that they probably *do* spend less time than do the dentists. The professors appear content with the amount of time they spend with their families.

8. Rolf B. Meyersohn, "Social Research in Television," in *Mass Culture* (Bernard Rosenberg and David M. White, eds.; Glencoe: The Free Press, 1957), p. 345.

9. David Riesman, in commenting upon this finding, has suggested the importance of the differential cultural approval of work: there being little ambivalence concerning academic work, the wives and children must put up with it.

10. Cf. Herbert Collins, "The Sedentary Society," in *Mass Leisure, op. cit.,* pp. 19-30.

11. While most of the professors and two-thirds of the admen have a high proportion of colleagues among their best friends, only 20 per cent of the dentists do. See Joel E. Gerstl, "Determinants of Occupational Community in High Status Occupations," *The Sociological Quarterly,* II (January, 1961), 37-48.

12. Morris Axelrod, "Urban Structure and Social Participation," *American Sociological Review,* 21 (February, 1956), p. 16. In the Detroit area, association with relatives is reported as: 49 per cent at least once a week, 13 per cent a few times a month, 12 per cent about once a month, 22 per cent less often. For association with friends, the figures are: 28 per cent at least once a week, 19 per cent a few times a month, 18 per cent about once a month, and 31 per cent less often. Part of the difference between these figures on friends and ours is due to Axelrod's data not including neighbors as friends. More importantly, there is no reason to expect our three high status occupational groups to resemble an urban cross-section.

13. Theater and concert attendance will be considered subsequently.

14. It should be noted that attendance at sports events is a different matter for the professors since all their attendance, with one or two exceptions, refers to Sauk sports. The professors in attending these events are not necessarily displaying their enthusiasm for sports, but rather for the glory of Sauk.

15. All the Catholic respondents claimed weekly church attendance, while the two Jewish ones attended only several times a year. This makes the appropriate occupational contrast one between Protestant respondents.

16. Over two-thirds of the dentists rated themselves as one of the top three occupations from a list of eleven consisting of: physician, business executive, lawyer, scientist, minister, architect, journalist, foreign service diplomat, dentist, adman, college professor. None of the admen or professors placed the dentists in the top three. See Joel E. Gerstl, *op. cit.* An open-ended social class question produced the following results:

Social Class	Admen	Dentists	Professors
Lower-middle, Middle, Common, or "Not Society"	32%	84%	72%
Upper-middle, Lower-upper	60	12	8
Don't know, Are no classes	8	4	20

17. Civic commitments include: the Citizens League, a hospital board, the Citizen's Committee for Education, the National Council of Christians and Jews, the NAACP Board, a township citizen's council, a Republican precinct chairmanship, the Chamber of Commerce, and several other businessmen's groups. In addition, memberships in youth service groups tend to be at the executive levels of such organizations as the YMCA or Big Brothers. (Dentists active in youth service were mainly referring to PTA and local scouting groups.)

18. See the social class distribution in footnote 16. While the admen do not rate their occupational prestige as low as they are rated by professors and dentists, in conformity with the pervasive tendency to overestimate the status of one's own occupation, they accord themselves a fairly low status and are very conscious of their even lower status in the eyes of outsiders.

19. The social background of wives is no doubt relevant in this context. (The respondents in the three occupations had similar backgrounds.) There is a decided tendency for dentists to have married "less well" than either of the other two groups. Whereas three-fourths of both admen and professors married the daughters of managers-proprietors or professionals, none of the dentists was married to professionals' daughters and only one-fourth of their wives had managerial-proprietor fathers; 45 per cent had blue-collar fathers. Similarly, most of the dentists' wives did not attend college, while wives of admen and professors did.

20. Russell Lynes, *The Tastemakers* (New York: Harper and Brothers, 1955).

21. Obviously this brow measure is a crude one. It might be argued that to attend theater is not upper brow if the show is a banal musical comedy. Even more serious would be the charge that the brow of the book-reader could only be ascertained according to the nature of the book read. Certainly I would want to make such distinctions if the present "instrument" were to be elaborated. In the present context, however, I would argue that to read books—regardless of content—is higher brow than not to read books at all. Similarly, even bad theater involves exposure to a range of experience different from even the best of TV. For some insightful comments concerning brows (if not their measurement) see, Edward Shils, "Mass Society and Its Culture," and Ernest Van den Haag, "A Dissent from the Consensual Society," *Daedalus* 89 (Spring, 1960), pp. 288-324.

22. Some magazines would have to be omitted due to their cross-brow nature, *Time* and *Newsweek* being prime examples.

23. An additional problem which has not been considered is that of occupational selection. It is not merely occupational milieu that

explains behavior, but occupational choice that selects personality and skills. The man who lacks manual dexterity is unlikely to manage to graduate from dental school. Avenues of vocational training are also important through the development of trained incapacities or compensations for various types of shortcomings. David Riesman, in a private communication, suggested that the dentists in order to get through their long training may have become somewhat cut off from people and therefore more oriented to family and do-it-yourself. Similarly, the professors might have turned to academic work as a retreat from their inabilities in sports as early as high school. But for the purposes of the present analysis, incumbency in the occupational role is taken as given.

ROBERT S. WEISS
Brandeis University

DAVID RIESMAN
Harvard University

9

Some Issues in the Future of Leisure*

WE WANT IN THIS ARTICLE to explore some of the problems in the use of the leisure which technological and organizational development have brought within our reach. Primarily, we shall be concerned with the consequences for the industrial worker of the new phase of the Industrial Revolution in which the level of productivity for mass-produced articles is almost independent of the input of human energy, and leisure consequently is available to just those men who might once have found themselves condemned to endless days in the plant. Secondarily, we shall be concerned with the consequences for members of the professional and managerial stratum of a shift in our cultural climate by which work seems to have lost some of its centrality, although the hours of work demanded of professionals and managers, and the psychic arduousness of their tasks have declined little, if at all.

Work and Leisure for the Industrial Workers

It is a political and economic problem to ensure that leisure be the consequence of technological developments, and not simply unemployment. This first, and basic, problem is far from solved. Wage protection alone is not the answer, although

---

* Reprinted from *Social Problems*, Vol. 9, No. 1, Summer, 1961.

Galbraith has cogently argued[1] for maintaining the purchasing power of the unemployed at almost the level they realized while employed. Such a measure fails to give to men the structuring of the day, the feeling of personal adequacy, and the relatedness to society that only work provides for most adult male Americans. It is true that if industrial workers are asked in a survey why a job is important, they tend to respond with matter-of-fact phrases like "You have to work to eat," or "That's the way the society works." Yet these conventional remarks cover the fact that for most of them holding down a job is necessary to a sense of responsible, and respectable, adulthood.[2] Not only do they feel that it is a man's role, in a timeworn phrase, "To bring home the bacon," but a sizeable minority of them believe that marriage is important because it provides a man with a family for whom he may work.[3] (A paradoxical reversal of the image of the man trapped into marriage and a life of servitude.) To be sure, there are exceptions in those groups and communities which have adapted to widespread, endemic unemployment. Young single men awaiting military service are often at a disadvantage in seeking employment; occasionally, having dropped out of school, they may seek to prove their manliness by what is ironically called juvenile delinquency. So too those discriminated against in the job market, such as Negroes and Puerto Ricans in Harlem, may find other patterns of masculinity.

In a society where most men work, the job furnishes a metronome-like capacity to keep in order one's routine of waking and sleeping, time on and time off, life on and life off the job. As surveys show, however, only a minority of industrial workers have any interest in the jobs themselves: it would be amazing to find a job so satisfying that a man would be anxious to continue with it after the day is over. Occasionally a skilled machinist will take a dour pride in his ability to turn out a blue-printed piece, or in his ingenuity in outwitting the time study man, but these accomplishments seldom suffice to sustain his interest during a long day spent setting and nursing a turret lathe. Moreover, as Robert Dubin has argued, not even the community that springs up on the shop floor is of great moment to the production workers,[4] although his membership in it and liking for it may be essential in permitting him to get through the day.[5] His relations with his fellows are neither deep nor necessarily permanent. No matter how friendly the work group to which he belongs, the industrial worker is unlikely to stay on a job simply because of his group membership; instead, he is likely to assume that his next job will furnish him with an equally good group of men to work with. Save in the form of car pools, work contacts are almost never carried off the job. (Not that this is necessarily regrettable: contacts off the job may be regarded as all the more refreshing because they differ or appear to differ from those on the job.)

Given the lack of intrinsic interest in work, it is not surprising that during the last century the lower ranks of industrial and office workers have taken part of the gains of productivity in the form of time off rather than in the form of increased pay. Up to a certain point, this drive to reduce hours is a drive also to increase one's chances to be human: but when waking time outside of work comes to equal or exceed waking time at work, the marginal utility of further free time or unpaid time may come into question. Even so, the drive to reduce hours continues. Perhaps it is partly maintained by the sheer momentum of the revolution by which the working class has become the new leisure class; partly by the growing cynicism regarding the intrinsic worth of any work, which is noted by Paul Goodman in *Growing Up Absurd*[6]; and partly by the high hopes of what a holiday may bring, which is to be found among those who like many workers as well as many school children, are thoroughly bored with what they normally do; and justified always by the need to spread the work as a response to automation. Indeed, in the light of the purposes a job serves, reduction in the hours spent at work does not require any redefinition of the importance of work: so long as one has a job, requiring some substantial fraction of time, work has met its most important requirement for the industrial worker. Yet when free time is empty and resembles a temporary layoff more than it does an anticipated weekend, men begin to be restless; many complain that the day is filled by small tasks requested by their wives.

It seems to us that the reduction of the work week may, for many men, be coming increasingly close to the point where it is not so much a matter of giving a disliked employer less for more, than it is a matter of getting more "free" time than one knows what to do with.

One development, of course, anticipated by Veblen, has postponed this day of reckoning; namely, that free time is time to expose oneself to all the stimuli for acquiring new consumer taste, which in turn requires new sources of income. Certainly increased leisure does not reduce financial need, and, where the six-hour day has been introduced, many men have taken on second jobs.[7] The unions are sharply opposed to the practice, on ideological grounds, since it defeats the aim of a reduced work week for members, and on practical grounds, since it means there are then fewer jobs to go around. Yet the practice is insidious, and in union circles, it is whispered that even union officials have taken on a second job as a real estate agent or bartender or cab driver. The most obvious explanation, and the one offered by union officials, is that the men are "money-hungry" and certainly the increasing rain of commercial appeals on all members of the family encourages a creeping inflation of desires. But this is, by itself, an insufficient explanation. These same men would object violently to working on holidays such as the Fourth of July, let alone Christmas, irrespective of double or triple time wages. Few of them, we would guess, would be willing to work seven days without a break, and most would object to having different days off instead of Saturday and Sunday. Rather, what has happened is that they have free time that is not clearly earmarked for leisure. It is as though their jobs suddenly turned from full-time to three-quarter time, and they must decide whether to loaf in that extra quarter time available or to go out and earn some money. And, given not only the desire for newer cars or refrigerators, but the indebtedness resulting from previous purchases, many members of this group could hardly help feeling that they had no right to work only part-time when, with only a little enterprise, they can find a second job which will bring them up to full-time. Nor are members of this group likely to catch up. There is a built-in cumulativeness about many consumer goods: the house can always be added to or improved; a car is a standing invitation to travel and to evenings out on the town; a television set, an invitational mirror of the good life. Continued reduction of the work week may yet come to mean for many men, not so much that they will give a disliked employer even less for more, but that they will again have gotten more free time than they know what to do with.

It is hard to see any way out of this spiral in the distribution of leisure to industrial workers. Given incomes inadequate to aspirations, and aggressive selling through the mass media and elsewhere, with resulting indebtedness, is it likely that the individual who is in debt will accept a thirty-hour or a twenty-hour week, without looking for another job? What indeed are the alternatives for him? He has now more time than necessary to recuperate from work's pressures or compensate for its demands: increase in the amount of leisure means that not only will there be more time for compensatory activities—to the extent that this is a primary function of leisure—but that there will be less need for such activities. Thus, recuperation from work's pressures as a rationale for the use of leisure time may no longer loom so large. Even if recuperation remains important, a man may decide that another job of a very different sort is just as "recreational" as one more evening spent bowling or looking at television or driving about.

An ironic commentary on the pressure toward a reduction in the workweek is provided by a study in which industrial workers were asked what they would do if they had an extra hour a day; most of them responded: "Sleep."[8] While for a few this may bespeak an over-full life, and for others a general irritation with a nettling or silly question, the answer seems to us to symbolize the lack of interests and resources that could give point to the leisure time that is now available. A study of the unpredictably scheduled to permit other employment on the additional day off, indicates that this additional day was less of a boon for the workers than they had originally anticipated.[9] The extra day off was not a day off for the children, so there was an empty house during school hours; nor was it a day off for the wife, so there was house-cleaning and vacuuming, with the man in the way. In this plant, a small aircraft manufacturing company in southern California, the four-day week was scheduled for one week out of four. Though originally anticipated with high hopes, it was soon disliked: television, loafing, ballgames, all these were felt to be week-end activities, and fell flat during the work week. One wonders whether, even in California, this reflects residual Puritanism, analogous to the feeling that it is wicked to go to the movies in the morning. It certainly does reflect the social or festive nature of much valued leisure, as well as the difficulty in developing a program for the use of a sizeable increase in leisure time when other members of the family and the community are not equally free.

When we talk of programming, in fact, we come to a characteristic which seems most common within working class groups: the lack of the middle class pattern of postponed gratification and planning ahead, if not actual contempt for it. Only a few of these men use increased leisure to prepare themselves for higher vocational tasks. Only a few turn out for union meetings, and fewer still evidence any interest in improving the lot of the occupational group to which they belong or in taking a hand in the decisions that may affect them in the future. So, too, Great Books courses or union education programs seem to attract few workers. This relative indifference has not always been the case here: in the period before the Civil War, energetic workmen, in a burst of enthusiasm for science and literacy, created and attended the Mechanics Institutes. Presently, our educational system tends to siphon off from the working class the more literate and ambitious, while at the same time there is lacking in this country for the most part the level of intensive secondary education that, in a country like Denmark or Japan, leads many workers to become active, life-long readers. Furthermore, the ideological appeals that drive some workers in a country like Yugoslavia to pursue educational and agitational tasks, have largely vanished from what is no longer a labor movement but a (somewhat shrinking) labor vested interest.

In this situation, most industrial workers appear to fall back on their families as the enclave within which leisure is to be spent. The long drive on Sunday, with its combination of aim-lessness and togetherness, is traditional in this group. Leisure time away from the family, "with the boys," is defined as time for blowing off steam, and is limited to what is thought to be physiologically and psychologically necessary. Of course, this is not the whole story. Many workers cultivate fairly expensive and time consuming hobbies, such as hunting. Some attend art classes for adults, and a handful may join the predominately middle class groups devoted to amateur music. A very few take part in voluntary associational activities; by and large these are staffed by the upper social strata.

It is discomforting to reflect on the complexity and scope of the programs that would be required to overcome this legacy of passivity and aimlessness. What sort of adult education program could meet these workers halfway in helping them plan their leisure in terms of life-long opportunities? What sort of change of perspective on the world and the self is required before muted and barely realized dissatisfactions can become a lever for individual development?

At the level of the society the problems are no less grave. Where the recreationist works for the public rather than the private sector, he has as little leverage at his disposal as the city planner has. One of us recently had the chance to observe the enormous resistance that developed in a small Vermont community to the idea of a recreation leader that the town should build a swimming pool as a war memorial rather than some monument: the project was fought by the town's elders as frivolous and a waste of money, in spite of the fact that the nearby rivers had become too polluted for swimming. Only an enormous civic effort finally carried the project through, and now "everyone" can see what a boon it is to children and their parents, to farmers and workers after a hot day, and to otherwise idle teenagers who can display themselves on the high dives, or if they swim well enough, make a little money and gain some sense of responsibility from helping act as life-guards around the pool. One consequence of the political weak-ness of public recreation is a tendency to over-ideologize particular leisure-time activities, exaggerating their importance and their potential contribution to individual character and the fabric of society. The President's campaign for physical fitness as a way of beating the Russians is an illustration. College sports may have suffered in the same way; it has repeatedly been shown, in novels and in the newspapers, that there is nothing particularly character-building about football or basketball. Yet it is hard to see how social forms adequate to the new leisure can be developed without an ideology that will mobilize people and strengthen the power of the few groups who are now concerned with the preservation of wilderness areas, the setting aside of land in our sprawling metropolitan belts for the play of adults and children, and the general release of resources other than commercial ones for experimentation and research in the field of leisure. In comparison with the organizational forms developed for the integration of work effort, there barely exist social forms for the utilization of leisure. In comparison with the organizational forms developed for the integration of work-effort, there barely exist the social forms within which the energies of leisure might be developed or even illustrated. Yet this observation evokes the image of the Boy Scouts or the YMCA, and the whole paradox of planning for the use of what is an uncommitted part of one's life. Leisure is supposed to be informal, spontaneous, and unplanned,[10] and is often defined as unobligated time, not only free of the job but free of social or civic obligations, moonlighting, or more or less requisite do-it-yourself activities. One result of this outlook, however, is to discourage whatever planning is possible (except, perhaps, in terms of the family, not always the optimal unit for leisure when one thinks of the development of its individual members). When we confront such problems, we are inclined to think that significant changes in the organization of leisure are not likely to come in the absence of changes in the whole society: in its work, its political forms, and its cultural style.

Leisure in the Business and Professional Strata

As we have indicated at the outset, your business and professional people cannot by and large look forward to a decreasing work week or decreasing work day; nevertheless, it is our im-

pression that there is a relative decline in the emotional loading
of on-the-job and off-the-job activities.[11] Less and less do men
in these strata behave as though, in Margaret Mead's terms,
"Leisure must be earned by work and good works . . . (and)
. . . while it is enjoyed it must be seen in a context of future
work and good works."[12] Instead, leisure becomes an opportunity
for what are being defined as the really important tasks of life:
care for home and family, service to the community, exploration
and gratification of the self. Thus, while work is losing its hold
on the time of the industrial worker, it is moderating its demands
on the interest and dedication of the business and professional
person. In fact, the familism of these latter strata comes more
and more to resemble that of the industrial worker.

Even so, there are still very large differences in different
occupations with respect to the centrality of work. Top managers,
as surveys and stories make clear, can still work sixty- and
seventy-hour weeks without feeling too remorseful about neglect
of domesticity. In contrast, physicians, college instructors school-
teachers may work equally long hours but without quite so good
a conscience about their neglect of their families and themselves. It is in these latter groups that one sees developing a
more complex concept of what one might do with one's life,
a concept that requires that individuals achieve self-realization
as well as a certain position in the community. Attention to
the family and to the community tend to become elements of
this new aim, though perhaps insufficient in themselves. What is
clear is that the individual who has only his work is thought
to be onesided, possibly sick and certainly unfortunate. Similar
attitudes may be spreading in the ranks of middle management,
where junior executives may realize that they are not indis-
pensable and that in an increasingly complex and bureaucratic
society, they may be fools to drive themselves only in order to
achieve a moderately greater income and vastly greater responsibilities.

But these tendencies are only incipient, and most business and
professional men view their work in terms of a career rather
than a job, and depend on their work, not only to structure
their day and to provide a minimal sense of adequacy, but for

a sense that they are living up to their potentialities and their education. In business, and in many professions, it is very difficult to prevent the invasion of leisure by career requirements. For example, cocktail parties may be necessary to cement work relationships; evening courses and summer seminars may be necessary to "keep up," let alone advance; and the full briefcase carried home at night tends to accompany professional and managerial responsibilities.

Undoubtedly, the middle class person is likely to have many greater resources for using his generally smaller quotient of leisure. He possesses the financial and intellectual resources for complex hobbycraft equipment, for attending lectures and concerts and art museums, for skin-diving and skiing, and for reading non-fiction (while his wife reads novels). He may also be prepared to invest time in the development of new skills because, despite the growth of fun morality, he is likely to retain a belief in long-range planning, and distant goals. Furthermore, unlike the industrial worker, he is likely to look for activities in which he may make new friends with similar interests, just as his sociability is more formal and less likely to be confined to the family. Yet these class differences should not be exaggerated. There are a great many businessmen who find no leisure activity of great interest although they, unlike the industrial worker, are apt to find their work engrossing. Many of these regard leisure as time to be spent with one's family, time which is dull, obligatory, but nevertheless important. This becomes all too clear when these men are forcibly retired and when, despite ample financial resources, they sometimes go to pieces much as do the unemployed. Many of them feel that release from work leaves a void, one not easily filled by recreational activities. A few manage to substitute voluntary unpaid work in civic and charitable affairs, but most lack the ability or flexibility or contacts to do this.[13]

There is also an ideology of anti-planning in these strata, corresponding to the ideology of anti-planning among working-class men. But, whereas the latter ideology opposes too intense planning for one's self, the former ideology opposes permitting one's life to be planned by others (except within the often very tightly planned organizations of which they are members), and so many in these strata would hardly welcome a government-sponsored program of planning for leisure such as we have mentioned above in connection with the industrial workers. Yet these men are often victims of poor phasing of the boon of leisure during their life-cycle. Had this phasing been planned it would have become apparent that leisure can be packaged in a great many ways: late entrance into the labor force, permitting longer education, or more time for decision about future occupation; shorter days on the job, permitting second jobs, serious commitment to voluntary organizations, longer commuting ranges, or a great deal of time regularly spent around the house; longer weekends, permitting excursions, or an extra day spent entirely at home; longer vacations, permitting travel, or the alternation of an educational period with a work period; early partial retirement, permitting an individual to begin devoting himself to a new activity, a new occupation, or a new relationship to or rejection of the world where things are going on.

Very likely, people have different rhythms or personal "seasons" of work and non-work which they should learn early in life and to which they should seek to adapt their careers. It seems likely to us that retirement will come ever earlier, certainly for the working class and probably for the executive class, as productivity marches on and as higher education spreads and suitable positions have to be found for presumptive members of the meritocracy.[14]

Of course, among the well-to-do, Veblenian motivations are not extinct, and the piling up of consumer goods (and playing the stock market as a form of moonlighting) still absorbs much energy. But for younger business and professional people who have always been reasonably comfortable and well-fixed, the acquiring of possessions seldom becomes a mania, and the acquisition of cars, new homes, and *objets d'art* cannot fill even the residual leisure. One symptom of the restlessness that this occasions is the uneasy flirtation being carried on, in some of these groups, with the ascetic ideology of national purpose.[15] Durkheim long ago noted that nationalism is the religion appropriate to the modern state, and increasingly political action organizations appear to be enlisting the free energies of the emotionally underemployed.[16] It has been observed many times that race riots are more common in the summer, primarily because people are out-of-doors and have nothing else to do. (Not that they decide to organize a race riot, but they become interested in what is going on, and go down to see, and things go on from there.) Southern picket lines in Little Rock and New Orleans appear to be made up in large part of housewives whose children are no longer young enough to be all-absorbing, and who are seeking to discover, in the process of its defense, a "way of life" that permits them to use their leisure in marches, telephone harassment of opponents, and meetings with comrades which provide a sense of personal worth and belongingness. When leisure is absorbed in this way, one can only wish momentarily that television, ordinarily the greatest single occupant of leisure time, could draw these people back to the Westerns and other melodramas.

In the best of our college students we see a use of leisure that is often admirable: instead of the fraternity make-work of an earlier day, there is serious concern with current issues, with reading and companionship, and often a strong interest in music, drama, literature and nature. We need only compare these students, products of affluence, intelligence and civility, with many of their parents to see that the future of leisure is not merely a dangerous abyss. The first well-to-do generation, whether in this country or elsewhere, often spends its leisure as it spends its riches (if it does not hoard both) with self-defeating aimlessness. We have seen new Americans, released from the poverty of peasant backgrounds, go on a buying spree and end up possessed by their possessions—nostalgically still hungering after a vanished good life after the manner of Gatsby in Fitzgerald's novel. Having just escaped from poverty, they are not yet ready to escape from freedom. And then we have seen their children, often to the third and fourth generation, wonder what to do when the simplicity of the older goals has been destroyed and their meaninglessness revealed by experience and by contemporary social criticism.

Yet, today, we find among the best of our students many who do not think of themselves as an ascribed elite or even an ambitiously achieving one: they are democratically oriented and they are capable of solidarity and social concern. In fact they *are* an elite, but one which by its nature, may show the way for others. The students may represent a pattern that will flourish, one that will break down the boundaries between work and leisure without getting rid of either.

NOTES

1. John Kenneth Galbraith, *The Affluent Society* (Boston: Houghton-Mifflin, 1958).

2. Material on the functions of work is based on a study by R. S. Weiss and R. L. Kahn, supported by a grant from the Institute of Labor and Industrial Relations, The University of Michigan—Wayne State University. See also R. S. Weiss and R. L. Kahn, "Definitions of Work and Occupation," *Social Problems*, 8 (Fall, 1960), pp. 142-51.

3. Based on unpublished results of a survey conducted by the Survey Research Center, University of Michigan, 1953.

4. Robert Dubin, "Industrial Workers' Worlds: A Study of the Central Life Interests of Industrial Workers," *Social Problems* (January, 1956), pp. 131-42. (Dubin's article also appears in this volume.)

5. Donald Roy, "Banana Time," *Human Organization,* Volume 18, No. 4 (Winter, 1959-60), pp. 158-68.

6. Paul Goodman, *Growing Up Absurd* (New York: Random House, 1960).

7. Harvey Swados. "Less Work—Less Leisure," in *Mass Leisure* (Eric Larrabee and Rolf Meyersohn, eds.; Glencoe, Illinois: Free Press, 1958), pp. 353-63.

8. Reported by Rolf Meyersohn.

9. Rolf Meyersohn, "Some Consequences of Changing Work and Leisure Routines" (paper presented to the Fourth Congress of Sociology, Section on Leisure, Milan-Strezza, Italy, September, 1959). (A revision of Meyersohn's paper appears in this volume.)

10. See, in this connection, David Riesman, Robert J. Potter, and Jeanne Watson, "Sociability, Permissiveness, and Equality," in *Psychiatry: Journal for the Study of Interpersonal Processes, Volume* 23, No. 4 (November, 1960), pp. 323-40; and by the same authors,

"The Vanishing Host," in *Human Organization,* Volume 19, No. 1 (Spring, 1960), pp. 17-27.

11. See, for two reports on the future aspirations of college students, David Riesman, "The Found Generation," *The American Scholar,* Vol. 25 (Fall, 1956); and David Riesman, "The College Student In an Age of Organization," *Chicago Review,* Vol. 12, No. 3 (Autumn, 1958), pp. 50-68.

12. Margaret Mead, "The Pattern of Leisure in Contemporary American Culture," in *Mass Leisure* (Eric Larrabee and Rolf Meyersohn, eds.; Glencoe, Illinois: Free Press, 1958), pp. 10-15.

13. See the comments on the retired in Alan Harrington, *Life in the Crystal Palace* (New York: Knopf, 1959).

14. Morris Janowitz, in a personal communication, predicts that as the society becomes more affluent, and there is increasing recognition of the elements contributing to the "good life," there will be more pressure for early retirement from those in industrial work. This will arise not from economic considerations, but in order to permit them time to "get something out of life" after years of unrewarding work.

15. Several years ago one of us (D.R.) got a letter out of the blue from a group of business and professional men in a small Midwestern community who asked about the John Birch Society because they wanted to devote themselves to the fight against communism. Upon receiving the reply that in their whole state there were probably no more than a dozen Communists, half of them likely FBI agents, and that there were a number of less exciting but more worthwhile tasks to be accomplished in their local community, they abruptly terminated the correspondence.

16. For its description of the way in which the well-to-do who would like to be considered natives in Santa Barbara, California, have joined the John Birch Society, see John D. Weaver, "Santa Barbara: Dilemma in Paradise," *Holiday,* Vol. 29, No. 6 (June, 1961), pp. 82-86.

PETER HENLE

United States Department of Labor,
Bureau of Labor Statistics

APPENDIX ARTICLE

10

Recent Growth of Paid
Leisure for U.S. Workers*

TRADITIONALLY, the American economy has been oriented more toward work than leisure. American habits of living and American cultural standards have tended to emphasize the virtues of work and the vices of idleness. Of course, in the Nation's earlier years, there was little choice; only through constant toil could the early settlers provide for themselves and their families. Long working hours were the accepted practice for the early industrial enterprises as well.

Gradually, a productive economy and a changing climate of public opinion made possible more leisure time. One of the primary goals of early union activity was a shorter workday and workweek. The value of rest away from work and the adverse effects on health of long hours became recognized. The accepted standard for hours of work declined slowly, through voluntary action by employers, collective bargaining, and State and Federal legislation. The 12-hour day gave way to the 10- and then the 8-hour standard, and eventually the 40-hour, 5-day week became the norm. A more recent development has been the emphasis on other forms of leisure—the paid vacation

---

* From the Monthly Labor Review, March, 1962.

and the paid holiday. Before World War II, these were quite limited for hourly paid workers, although many salaried workers had been receiving this type of benefit.

Increased leisure has also been a by-product of various shifts within the economy. The decline in employment in agriculture and small retail stores, both of which traditionally involve long hours, has meant an automatic drop in average working hours.

This growth of leisure time has played a major role in shifting the patterns of family living and in stimulating more widespread travel, sports, and recreation activity throughout the country. Much of the output of the American economy now consists of end products for leisure-time use or consumption. For example, while the gross national product grew by 14 per cent between 1957 and 1960, consumer expenditures for foreign travel were up 34 per cent; books and maps, 28 per cent; theater and opera, 26 per cent; and commercial participant amusements (such as bowling), 30 per cent.

The purpose of this article is to bring together statistics which the Bureau of Labor Statistics has compiled from time to time on various aspects of leisure time, primarily hours of work, paid vacations, and paid holidays. It also attempts, for the first time, to measure changes in the average worker's available leisure time in the 20 years 1940-60. In doing so, leisure time is not defined simply as time away from work because, in an economic sense, leisure has little meaning unless it represents paid time taken voluntarily. The individual concerned has to be assured that he can spend time away from work without sacrificing living standards for himself and his family. It is in this sense that leisure time is used in this article.

Hours of Work

Hours of work have been declining for over a century.[1] The most marked reductions occurred between 1900 and 1930, when average weekly hours dropped from about 67 to 55 in agriculture and from 56 to 43 for nonagricultural workers.

During the depression of the 1930's, working hours were further reduced, but by necessity rather than choice. Most of the industry codes promulgated under the National Industrial

Recovery Act between 1933 and 1935 included provisions limiting the workweek to 40 hours (in some cases, 35) in an effort to stimulate greater employment. The enactment of the Fair Labor Standards Act in 1938 represented legislative decision that 40 hours a week constituted a desirable standard, with certain exceptions, for workers in interstate commerce. Work after 40 hours was not prohibited, but was made expensive to schedule by requiring that such hours be paid for at the penalty rate of time and one-half. The new standard was introduced gradually, beginning with 44 hours for the first year of the new law. The 40-hour standard became effective in October, 1940, and at that time, workweeks exceeding this standard were found almost exclusively in industry groups either partially or wholly exempt from the Fair Labor Standards Act—retail trade and class I railroads, for example.

The most significant change since 1940 has been the more widespread adoption of the 40-hour week. Far more workers have seen their hours shortened to 40 than reduced below this level. While there have been some reductions of work schedules below 40 hours, these have taken place only in a few industries, largely those in which unions have made shorter hours a primary objective in collective bargaining. In effect, the standard set in the Fair Labor Standards Act for firms in interstate commerce had, by 1960, been extended to the vast majority of nonfarm wage and salary workers.[2]

These are conclusions reached after an examination of available BLS data on hours of work during the period 1940-60. Three types of data have been involved in this examination:

1. *Hours worked* by individuals in the labor force as reported by a sample of the Nation's households and published in the Monthly Report on the Labor Force. (Data for periods prior to July, 1959 were published by the Bureau of the Census.)

2. *Scheduled hours of work* as reported by employers in response to surveys of wage rates covering wage and salary workers in particular localities and industries.

3. *Straight-time hours* as reported by labor unions in four industries in which the Bureau conducts surveys of union scale wage rates.

The basic figures for average hours worked are shown in Table 1 for May of 1948, 1956, and 1960 for the various classes of workers in the economy. (Comparable data for earlier years are not available.) These months were chosen because they represent months of generally high economic activity. By choosing the same month of each year, problems of seasonal adjustment were avoided.

These figures make it clear that hours are still longer in agricultural than in nonagricultural pursuits. Moreover, those who set their own hours, the self-employed, work longer hours than those whose hours are set by their employer or through collective bargaining.

Between 1948 and 1960, average weekly hours worked by all employed persons declined by 2.6 hours, or 6 per cent. However, since part-time workers have been forming a considerably higher portion of the labor force, the figures for all workers exaggerate the trend toward a shorter workweek. In 1960, almost 6 million workers voluntarily were working at jobs of less than 35 hours a week.[3] The decline for full-time workers was only 1.3 hours, or 2.8 per cent. The drop in working hours for full-time workers was quite marked in

TABLE 1

Average Weekly Hours Worked by Persons at Work, 1948, 1956, and 1960

Class of worker	All Workers			Full-time workers[1]		
	May 1948	May 1956	May 1960	May 1948	May 1956	May 1960
Total at work	43.4	41.6	40.8	46.8	46.0	45.5
Agriculture	52.5	49.6	48.0	58.3	56.4	55.5
Wage and salary workers	49.4	42.8	43.3	56.9	53.5	52.3
Self-employed workers	57.9	58.7	56.5	59.6	59.2	58.6
Unpaid family workers	39.4	35.8	35.4	54.0	49.3	49.4
Nonagricultural industries	41.9	40.7	40.1	45.2	44.8	44.6
Wage and salary workers	41.1	39.7	39.3	44.2	43.8	43.7
Private employers	41.1	(2)	39.1	44.3	(2)	43.8
Government	41.3	(2)	40.3	43.1	(2)	43.1
Self-employed workers	47.9	49.1	47.1	52.7	53.1	52.7
Unpaid family workers	39.4	39.4	40.0	50.1	50.2	49.4

[1] Persons who worked 35 hours or more during the survey week.
[2] Not available.

agriculture; in fact, several times the decline for nonagricultural workers. On the other hand, there was no decline for full-time self-employed persons in nonagricultural industries.

The distribution of full-time wage and salary workers by hours worked in Table 2 confirms the continuing slow decline in the average workweek. Yet for most workers there has been little, if any, change in working hours. The majority of nonfarm workers were on a 40-hour workweek in 1948 and have remained so. By 1960, those working fewer than 40 hours had increased from 5 to 8 per cent of all full-time nonagricultural wage and salary workers. Each of the industry divisions also showed an increase in the proportion of those with workweeks of less than 40 hours. However, only in nondurable manufactures and the service, finance, insurance, and real estate division was this proportion higher than 10 per cent.

More significant perhaps was the drop in the proportion of those working more than 40 hours, from 43 per cent in 1948 to 33 per cent in 1960. The drop was sharpest for agriculture, where the proportion working 48 or more hours declined from 81 to 60 per cent. In manufacturing, where the 40-hour week was standard by 1940, the decline was slight; but in mining, transportation, trade, and services, the continuing shift toward the 40-hour week was quite marked.

These figures, of course, represent hours actually worked, as reported by a member of the households included in the survey. An individual working longer than 40 hours may be doing so because he has been assigned overtime work, because those are his regular hours, or because he has more than one job. (In December, 1960, 3 million workers held more than one job.[4]) Similarly, a person working 35-39 hours may have a work schedule calling for those hours, may have begun or quit a job during the survey week, or may have missed certain scheduled hours for such reasons as illness, bad weather, or cutbacks in production. However, the years selected were years of relatively high economic activity, so that differences in the amount of both overtime and short time would be slight. In any case, the definition of full-time workers as those working 35 hours or more would exclude most short-time workers. Moreover, the

TABLE 2

Full-Time Wage and Salary Workers, by Hours of Work During the Survey Week and Industry, May of 1948, 1952, 1956, and 1960

[Percent distribution]

May of—	Total, 35 hours or more	35 to 39 hours	40 hours	41 to 47 hours	48 hours or more
AGRICULTURE					
1948	100.0	3.6	10.7	5.2	80.5
1952	100.0	6.2	14.0	7.4	72.4
1956	100.0	7.9	13.6	10.7	67.8
1960	100.0	6.2	18.2	15.9	59.7
NONAGRICULTURAL INDUSTIES, TOTAL					
1948	100.0	4.8	51.8	12.3	31.1
1952	100.0	6.1	55.0	11.3	27.7
1956	100.0	7.4	56.3	11.1	25.2
1960	100.0	7.6	59.6	9.4	23.3
MINING					
1948	100.0	.7	41.8	5.4	52.1
1952	100.0	1.4	48.9	6.0	43.7
1956	100.0	3.5	56.3	8.7	31.5
1960	100.0	7.4	59.1	5.4	28.1
CONSTRUCTION					
1948	100.0	4.9	54.4	12.3	28.5
1952	100.0	4.8	54.9	9.6	30.7
1956	100.0	8.5	58.9	10.8	21.8
1960	100.0	6.9	64.8	10.0	18.3
MANUFACTURING, TOTAL					
1948	100.0	4.1	66.7	11.2	18.0
1952	100.0	5.7	65.5	10.1	18.7
1956	100.0	6.4	66.3	9.1	18.2
1960	100.0	6.7	68.4	8.2	16.7
Durable goods					
1948	100.0	2.2	68.7	12.4	16.7
1952	100.0	2.7	66.3	10.5	20.5
1956	100.0	3.6	68.3	9.0	19.2
1960	100.0	3.4	73.4	7.8	15.4
Nondurable goods					
1948	100.0	6.4	64.5	8.6	19.5
1952	100.0	9.9	64.3	9.6	16.7
1956	100.0	10.7	63.4	9.2	16.7
1960	100.0	11.0	61.7	8.8	18.4

(continued)

TABLE 2 (continued)

Full-Time Wage and Salary Workers, by Hours of Work During the Survey Week and Industry, May of 1948, 1952, 1956, and 1960

[Percent distribution]

May of—	Total, 35 hours or more	35 to 39 hours	40 hours	41 to 47 hours	48 hours or more
TRANSPORTATION AND PUBLIC UTILITIES					
1948	100.0	2.1	42.5	11.2	44.2
1952	100.0	2.8	65.9	7.1	24.3
1956	100.0	4.3	67.9	7.9	19.9
1960	100.0	4.3	69.3	6.8	19.6
WHOLESALE AND RETAIL TRADE					
1948	100.0	3.3	34.8	15.5	46.5
1952	100.0	4.2	36.5	16.8	42.4
1956	100.0	5.5	40.0	14.9	39.6
1960	100.0	6.1	44.1	13.0	36.8
SERVICES AND FINANCE [1]					
1948	100.0	10.3	40.8	13.8	35.1
1952	100.0	11.3	44.7	13.3	30.6
1956	100.0	12.3	45.6	13.4	28.7
1960	100.0	12.0	51.3	10.3	26.5
PUBLIC ADMINISTRATION					
1948	100.0	2.0	67.2	8.8	22.0
1952	100.0	4.7	68.5	6.0	20.7
1956	100.0	5.3	68.5	7.6	18.6
1960	100.0	4.8	71.3	6.3	17.6

[1] Includes insurance and real estate.

proportion of multiple jobholders has not changed significantly.[5] Consequently, there is little doubt that the 1948-60 decline in hours worked reflected, for the most part, changes in scheduled hours.

These figures on hours actually worked can be compared with BLS studies providing data on scheduled hours. Such figures for the year ending June 30, 1961, are available for 13.8 million workers in the country's standard metropolitan areas (Table 3).[6] Almost two-thirds of all office workers and over four-fifths of all plant workers in metropolitan areas were employed in establishments in which a 40-hour schedule predominated. Practically all the remaining office workers had schedules of less than 40 hours (mostly 35 or 37½), while most of the other plant workers had hours longer than 40. As a general rule, office workers had shorter scheduled hours than plant workers.

The figures for scheduled hours generally fall below those for hours actually worked by full-time workers but follow a similar pattern of industry variations. The incidence of overtime work and dual jobholding would tend to make working hours longer than scheduled hours. In addition, the scheduled hours data cover only metropolitan areas, where hours are often shorter than in the smaller cities and rural areas.

No comparable information on scheduled hours is available for years prior to 1960, but the Bureau's union wage-scale studies provide hours information dating back to earlier years for four industries (Table 4).

In the printing trades, nearly all unions have succeeded in their attempts to reduce scheduled hours below 40. In 1940, 64 per cent of the union workers in the industry were scheduled to work a 40-hour week, while only 13 per cent had workweeks below 37½. By 1960, only 2 per cent were on a 40-hour week, while 54 per cent had schedules of less than 37½ hours. The average workweek had dropped to 36.6 hours.

In the local trucking and transit industries, unions have achieved widespread reductions in the workweek to the standard 40 hours. In trucking, 65 per cent of union members in 1940 worked schedules of 48 hours or more. By 1960, this figure had been reduced to 2 per cent while the proportion working 40 hours or less had grown from 13 to 94 per cent. While 1940 data for the local transit industry are not available, the trend from 1946 to 1960 is similar. In the earlier year, almost as many union members were working 48 or more hours as were working the 40-hour week. By 1960, only 4 per cent had schedules as long as 48 hours, while 85 per cent were on the 40-hour week.

In the fourth industry—construction—the average schedule has actually lengthened somewhat since 1940, when 29 per cent of the workers were still on schedules that had been shortened below 40 hours during the depression of the 1930's. During World War II, standard hours in many areas were lengthened to the 40-hour week, and this standard has been generally maintained in the postwar years. As a result, in 1960, only 12 per cent of the workers were on schedules of less than 40 hours.

TABLE 3

Work Schedules of First-Shift Plant and Office Workers in Metropolitan Areas,[1] by Industry Division, Year Ending June 30, 1961

[Per cent of workers]

Scheduled weekly hours	All indus- tries	Manu- fac- turing	Public util- ities[2]	Whole- sale trade	Retail trade	Fi- nance[3]	Serv- ices[4]
Office Workers							
All schedules	100	100	100	100	100	100	100
Under 40 hours[5]	35	21	23	29	23	64	49
35 hours	10	7	9	9	5	17	18
36¼ hours	3	1	(6)	2	2	8	3
37½ hours	13	8	13	13	10	21	19
38¾ hours	4	4	1	3	2	7	4
40 hours	64	78	76	66	70	36	46
Over 40 hours	2	1	(6)	5	7	(6)	5
Average hours	38.9	39.4	39.2	39.2	39.6	37.9	38.6
Plant Workers							
All schedules	100	100	100	100	100		100
Under 40 hours[5]	7	7	1	4	10		8
37½ hours	3	3	1	2	4		3
40 hours	82	85	94	77	67		63
Over 40 hours[5]	11	8	6	19	23		29
42 hours	1	1	1	1	2		2
44 hours	2	1	(6)	4	5		4
45 hours	2	2	2	3	3		3
48 hours	4	2	1	3	7		16
Over 48 hours	2	2	1	4	2		1
Average hours	40.5	40.2	40.3	41.1	41.1		41.5

[1] See text footnote 6.

[2] Includes transportation and communications. Railroads were excluded in a few of the areas studied.

[3] Includes insurance and real estate.

[4] Includes, among others, hotels, personal services, business services, auto-repair shops, motion pictures, nonprofit membership organizations, and engineering and architectural services.

[5] Includes weekly schedules other than those shown separately.

[6] Less than 0.5 per cent.

TABLE 4

Union Scales of Weekly Hours[1] in Selected Industries and Trades, Selected Dates, 1940-60

[Per cent of workers]

Hours scale[1]	Local trucking			Building trades			Printing trades			Local transit[2]		
	June 1940	July 1950	July 1960	June 1940	July 1950	July 1960	June 1940	July 1950	July 1960	July 1946[3]	July 1950	July 1960
All scales	100.0	100.0	100.0	100.0	100.0	100.0	100.0	100.0	100.0	100.0	100.0	100.0
Under 40 hours	0.4	0.9	3.0	29.2	13.5	12.0	35.5	85.9	97.8			
Under 35 hours				9.6	.9	1.2	4.1	2.2	2.3			
35 hours			1.4	19.6	12.6	10.7	5.0	6.4	19.1			
Over 35 and under 37½ hours			1.6				3.4	33.0	32.8			
37½ hours			1.6				21.7	42.6	43.1			
Over 37½ and under 40 hours			1.6				1.3	1.7	.5			
40 hours	12.7	72.1	91.1	66.9	86.5	88.0	63.8	13.9	2.2	31.6	31.9	84.7
Over 40 and under 48 hours	21.9	6.7	3.6	2.9	(⁴)	(⁴)	⁵.7	⁵.2		26.2	24.0	6.3
Over 40 and under 44 hours	5.3	1.3	1.1							4.0	5.4	1.7
44 hours	12.5	1.8	1.1							22.0	18.4	3.7
Over 44 and under 48 hours	4.1	3.6	2.5							.2	.2	.9
48 hours	44.4	16.7	2.0	.9						27.0	25.6	3.2
Over 48 hours	20.6	3.4	.1	(⁴)						3.7	3.7	.8
Not specified		.2	.2							11.5	14.8	5.0
Average hours	47.2	42.0	40.1	38.3	39.3	39.3	38.8	37.2	36.6	43.9	43.9	40.6

[1] Maximum schedules of hours at straight-time rates agreed upon through collective bargaining between trade unions and employers in cities of 100,000 or more.

[2] Operating employees only.

[3] Earliest date for which figures are available.

[4] Less than 0.05 per cent.

[5] May include a very small number with longer hours.

In summary, recent years have witnessed a gradual increase in leisure time through reductions in the standard workweek and in hours actually worked. While such reductions have taken place throughout the economy, they have not followed a uniform pattern. In a few industries, notably printing and publishing and women's apparel, general reductions in hours to a level below 40 have taken place. In many predominantly white-collar industries, the workday has also been reduced below 8 hours. In most manufacturing industries, the 40-hour week has remained standard. In such nonmanufacturing industries as retail trade and services, where many establishments were not subject to the Fair Labor Standards Act, there has been a major movement toward the 40-hour standard.

Paid Vacations

A more pervasive increase in leisure time since 1940 has occurred as paid vacations have been adopted or lengthened for virtually all types of workers.[7] For example, in 1940, collective bargaining agreements applying to 2 million organized wage earners, or about one-fourth of all union members, provided annual vacations with pay.[8] For most of these workers, the maximum vacation period for which they might become eligible was 1 week. A few agreements provided a 2-week vacation for all workers and about a fourth of the workers who got vacations were entitled to 2 weeks if they met specified service requirements, but only rarely was provision made for more than 2 weeks. By contrast in 1957, 91 per cent of the workers covered by major collective bargaining agreements (each covering 1,000 or more workers) were eligible for paid vacations, and 84 per cent of the agreements made provision for a maximum vacation of at least 3 weeks, usually for longer service employees.[9]

Practically all office and plant workers in the country's metropolitan areas are now entitled to paid vacations. In 1961, more extensive vacation benefits were generally provided for office than for plant workers. After 25 years of service, 38 per cent of the office employees but only 25 per cent of plant employees were eligible for 4 weeks or more of vacation

(Table 5). Similarly, after 10 years of service, 41 per cent of the office employees but only 29 per cent of the plant workers were eligible for 3 or more weeks of vacation. The most prevalent service requirements for the 2-week vacation were 1 year for office employees and 2 or 3 years for plant workers.

These figures, however, do not indicate the length of vacation actually taken by employees, and no such data are collected. But the Monthly Report on the Labor Force provides an estimate of the number of individuals absent from their job "on vacation" during the entire survey week. On the assumption that the survey week is representative of the months concerned, these data yield annual estimates of full weeks of vacation. (See Table 6.) For 1960, over 83 million full weeks of vacation were recorded—150 per cent of the 1948 level and an average of 1.3 weeks of vacation per employed person.

This figure understates total vacation time for two reasons: (1) The survey week, being the week ending nearest the 15th of the month, generally avoids all major holidays, whereas vacations tend to occur more frequently during holiday weeks. (2) The figure does not include paid vacation time of less than a full week. Including estimates for these two gaps in the calculations, a rough figure for total vacation time for 1960 would amount to 96-100 million vacation weeks.[10]

Almost 85 per cent of nonagricultural wage and salary workers were paid while on vacation in 1960. The percentage varied somewhat by industry, from a low of 60-70 per cent for construction and the service industries (including educational services) to 93 per cent for workers in transportation and public utilities and 96 per cent for employees in public administration.[11]

Paid Holidays

A similar development in recent years leading toward increased leisure has been the growth in the provision of time off with full pay on holidays.

Before World War II, while major holidays were frequently observed throughout industry, the practice of providing pay for hourly rated employees was quite rare. During the war, the practice of paid holidays first began to spread, partly as a

TABLE 5

Vacation Pay Provisions[1] for Office and Plant Workers in Metropolitan Areas,[2] by Industry Division, Year Ending June 30, 1961

[Per cent of workers]

Amount of vacation pay and length of service[1]	Office workers							Plant workers					
	All industries	Manufacturing	Public utilities[3]	Wholesale trade	Retail trade	Finance[4]	Services[5]	All industries	Manufacturing	Public utilities[3]	Wholesale trade	Retail trade	Services[5]
All provisions	100	100	100	100	100	100	100	100	100	100	100	100	100
After 1 Year of Service													
Under 1 week	([6])	([6])	([6])	([6])	([6])	([6])	([6])	1	1	([6])	([6])	1	([6])
1 week	23	16	53	26	63	3	25	73	77	64	59	69	70
Over 1 and under 2 weeks	1	1	([6])	([6])	([6])	([6])	1	4	6	2	([6])	2	2
2 weeks	75	80	46	72	35	96	70	18	13	31	36	27	18
Over 2 weeks	2	2	([6])	1	([6])	([6])	3	2	2	2	1	([6])	2
After 5 Years of Service													
Under 2 weeks	1	1	([6])	1	2	([6])	3	5	5	([6])	6	6	14
2 weeks	85	88	95	89	81	79	66	82	83	94	84	74	74
Over 2 and under 3 weeks	5	3	([6])	2		11	8	5	7	1	2	2	2
3 weeks	9	7	4	7	15	9	19	6	4	4	7	17	2
Over 3 weeks	([6])	([6])	([6])	([6])	([6])	([6])	3	([6])	([6])	([6])	([6])	([6])	1
After 10 Years of Service													
Under 2 weeks	1	1	([6])	1	2	([6])	3	4	3	([6])	4	6	14
2 weeks	50	47	71	52	41	46	47	48	45	71	54	39	61
Over 2 and under 3 weeks	8	13	3	3	1	9	1	18	26	3	4	1	3
3 weeks	40	38	25	42	53	44	42	27	23	24	34	51	14
Over 3 weeks	1	1	1	1	2	([6])	6	2	2	1	1	3	1

After 15 Years of Service

Under 2 weeks	1	1	(6)	1	2	(6)	3	4	3	(6)	4	6	14
2 weeks	15	13	5	25	26	12	27	19	16	3	29	28	44
Over 2 and under 3 weeks	1	1	(6)	1	1	(6)	1	2	3	(6)	1	(6)	2
3 weeks	79	81	92	71	69	80	60	69	71	92	62	61	32
Over 3 weeks	5	4	2	2	3	7	9	5	5	4	2	4	3

After 25 Years of Service

Under 2 weeks	1	1	(6)	1	2	(6)	3	4	3	(6)	4	6	14
2 weeks	13	12	5	24	24	9	25	17	15	3	28	26	42
Over 2 and under 3 weeks	(6)	1	(6)	(6)	(6)	(6)	1	2	3	(6)	1	(6)	2
3 weeks	46	49	56	43	24	42	50	43	44	56	43	32	31
Over 3 and under 4 weeks	3	6	1	1	1	1	1	7	11	1	1	(6)	1
4 weeks	37	31	38	30	50	47	19	25	22	38	22	36	5
Over 4 weeks	1	(6)	(6)	(6)	(6)	2	(6)	(6)	(6)	1	(6)	(6)	(6)

[1] Includes percentage or flat-sum type payments converted to equivalent weeks of pay. Periods of service were arbitrarily chosen and do not necessarily reflect the individual provisions for progression. For example, the changes in proportions indicated at 10 years' service include changes in provisions occurring between 5 and 10 years.

The distribution does not indicate the number of workers actually receiving vacations of the stipulated length, since this depends on the number meeting length-of-service and other eligibility requirements.

[2] See text footnote 6.
[3] See footnote 2, Table 3.
[4] See footnote 3, Table 3.
[5] See footnote 4, Table 3.
[6] Less than 0.5 per cent.

TABLE 6

Estimated Number of Full Vacation Weeks of Employed Persons, 1948, 1952, 1956, 1960

Item	1948	1952	1956	1960
Number of full vacation weeks (millions)	[1] 55.5	59.9	71.5	83.5
During July and August	[1] 36.5	36.2	42.0	49.4
During other 10 months	19.0	23.7	29.5	34.1
Average number of persons employed (millions)	59.1	61.0	64.7	66.7
Average number of vacation weeks per employed person	.9	1.0	1.1	1.3

[1] Survey week in July included July 4.

result of decisions by the National War Labor Board that the granting of as many as 6 paid holidays would be allowed within wage stabilization regulations. But in 1943, a Bureau of Labor Statistics analysis of collective bargaining contracts concluded:

> Although an increasing number of union agreements make provision for paying wage earners for some or all of the major holidays, the majority of agreements in manufacturing, construction, and mining merely provide time off on holidays, without pay.[12]

After the war, the practice of paid holidays spread generally throughout industry. The most recent sruvey of holiday provisions in major collective bargaining agreements indicated that in 1958 only 12 per cent of the workers covered were not entitled to paid holidays.[13] Nearly three-fifths of the workers under agreements calling for paid holidays were entitled to 7 or more paid holidays.

Currently, the average appears to be about 7 paid holidays in major American industries. In the country's metropolitan areas, data for 1961 show that all but 1 per cent of the office workers and 5 per cent of the plant workers received pay for holidays not worked (Table 7). The majority of both office and plant workers received 7 or more paid holidays. Some 24 per cent of the office employees had 9 or more paid holidays, but only 7 per cent of the plant workers received this number.

The average among those receiving holiday pay was 7.8 paid holidays for office workers and 7.0 for plant workers. Thus, the traditional advantage of office workers over plant workers with regard to this benefit still applies.

The number of paid holidays varied by industry. Traditionally, banks have had a liberal holiday policy, and over half of the office workers in the finance industry received 9 or more paid holidays, and over one-third, 11 or more. Among plant workers, the industry with the most extensive paid holiday provisions was public utilities. Among both office and plant employees, retail trade provided the fewest paid holidays.

TABLE 7

Paid Holiday Provisions[1] for Office and Plant Workers in Metropolitan Areas,[2] by Industry Division, Year Ending June 30, 1961

[Per cent of workers]

Number of paid holidays[1]	All indus-tries	Manu-factur-ing	Public utili-ties[3]	Whole-sale trade	Re-tail trade	Fi-nance[4]	Serv-ices[5]
Office Workers							
All provisions	99	99	99	99	98	99	98
Less than 6	4	2	1	7	10	5	8
6 and 6½	19	14	9	26	42	18	20
7 and 7½	33	49	47	24	32	10	20
8 and 8½	19	22	21	23	7	15	19
9 or more	24	12	22	20	7	51	21
Average number[6]	7.8	7.4	7.8	7.5	6.7	8.9	7.4
Plant Workers							
All provisions	95	96	98	97	93		77
Less than 6	8	5	2	13	18		18
6 and 6½	21	15	12	27	40		35
7 and 7½	44	52	49	23	22		14
8 and 8½	16	17	18	19	10		4
9 or more	7	6	16	14	4		6
Average number[6]	7.0	7.1	7.6	7.1	6.1		6.1

[1] All combinations of full and half days that add to the same amount are combined; for example, the proportion of workers receiving a total of 7 days includes those with 7 full days and no half days, 6 full days and 2 half days, 5 full days and 4 half days, etc.

[2] See text footnote 6.

[3] See footnote 2, Table 3.

[4] See footnote 3, Table 3.

[5] See footnote 4, Table 3.

[6] Based on workers in establishments providing paid holidays.

Frequently, the additional paid holidays that have been recognized have been, not the traditional holidays, but days that provide additional leisure time at certain times of the year or a longer weekend. For example, holidays immediately preceding Christmas and New Year's Day have become increasingly popular. The Friday following Thanksgiving has become a recognized holiday in a small number of bargaining agreements. Following are two agreement clauses which illustrate how the selection of holidays has been geared to the desires of employees for longer weekends.

> Washington's Birthday is designated as the holiday in February except when the observance of Lincoln's Birthday would provide a longer weekend, in which event Lincoln's Birthday shall be the observed holiday . . .

*   *   *   *

If Christmas Day is on—	The eighth holiday will be—
Sunday	Preceding Friday
Monday	Preceding Friday
Tuesday	Preceding Monday
Wednesday	Day after Thanksgiving
Thursday	Preceding Friday
Friday	Preceding Thursday
Saturday	Preceding Friday[14]

How Much More Leisure?

Clearly there has been a marked increase in leisure time over the past 20 years. Admittedly, estimates of how much increase has taken place must be rough approximations, particularly since few data are available for 1940. Nevertheless, they give for the first time some indication of the magnitude of changes in paid leisure time. Essentially, the increase in leisure time in 1960 over 1940[15] consists of the following:

	Hours per year per full-time employed person
1½ hours less in the workweek	75
6 days more paid vacation	48
4 days more paid holidays	32
Total	155

For the economy as a whole, this addition leisure time amounts to over 10 billion hours (5.0 billion from the shorter workweek, 3.2 billion in additional vacation, and 2.1 billion in added holidays).

Many of these hours represent additional time away from work. This is obviously true, for example, of the reduction in the workweek. However, the additional paid holidays largely represent payment for time which in 1940 was spent away from the plant without compensation. The additional vacation time is a combination of these two factors.

The 155 hours represent almost 4 average weeks of employment, but they represent only a small fraction of the gain in productivity that the national economy has achieved since 1940. BLS estimates of output per man-hour would indicate that to produce the 1960 output with the 1940 productivity would have required an additional 1,447 hours of working time—or 71 per cent more—for each employed member of the 1960 labor force.[16] Thus, the 155 hours that have been accounted for in terms of reduced hours of work, increased vacations, and paid holidays amount to only 11 per cent of the hours that have been made available by the Nation's increased productivity since 1940.

While this gain in leisure time represents only a relatively small proportion of the increased productivity since 1940, this is not unexpected. Much of the limited productivity gains of the previous decade, 1930-40, were reflected in shorter hours of work, not because workers preferred greater leisure but because of the depressed conditions of the decade. The passage of the Fair Labor Standards Act to a large extent reflected changes in hours that had already taken place. In the two decades following the 1930's, the emphasis quite naturally was on income rather than leisure.

A review of the changes in paid leisure between 1940 and 1960 shows that there was no major shift in the standard workweek. Perhaps the most significant development was that more than half the total gain in paid leisure resulted from increased vacation and holiday time, rather than from a reduction in working hours. This is a definite shift from the pattern of earlier years and seems to indicate that leisure time preferences are running more to additional whole days each year rather than additional minutes each day.

Of course, the leisure time gained since 1940 does not necessarily represent time available for travel, recreation, etc. The nature of the economy and the Nation's living habits have changed in important ways since 1940, and since individuals now live farther from their place of employment, some of this additional "leisure" time may now be spent in commuting to and from work.

Although the average employee has more leisure time today than in 1940, many individuals continue to prefer more work to more leisure in order to maximize their income. The operation of today's economy makes it possible for those who wish to work longer hours to do so, either by accepting overtime when it is available or by obtaining a second job. The economy also makes it possible for more people, especially women, to work at part-time jobs.

It is difficult to generalize about future trends in leisure time from this record. There is no way to measure the intensity of the demand for more leisure time against the intensity of the demand for greater income to be spent on leisure time activities. Trade unions continue to present demands for a shorter work-week, although much union pressure in this direction is motivated not by the desire for more leisure but by the possibility of increasing the number of jobs. Of course, regardless of the motivation, the attainment of shorter hours of work would bring with it greater leisure time.

Changes in vacation and holiday practices continue to be negotiated in collective bargaining. A number of unions have also expressed interest in some type of extended paid leave provided periodically for longer service employees.

One new factor is the form which the demands for leisure time are likely to take. The relatively slight decline in average hours of work in recent years has been accompanied by a greater interest in more extended paid vacations and a greater number of paid holidays. Providing a greater number of days off seems likely to continue to receive greater emphasis than reducing the time spent each day at work.

NOTES

1. "The Workweek in American Industry, 1850-1956," *Monthly Labor Review*, January, 1958, pp. 23-29.

2. A 1961 amendment to the Fair Labor Standards Act extended coverage to about 3.6 million workers, most of whom are in retail, service, and construction industries. Beginning September 3, 1963, most newly covered workers must be paid overtime after 44 hours, 1 year later, after 42 hours, and in 1965, after 40 hours.

3. "Labor Force and Employment in 1960," *Monthly Labor Review*, April, 1961, pp. 344-354.

4. "Multiple Jobholders in December 1960," *Monthly Labor Review*, October, 1961, pp. 1066-73.

5. *Ibid.*

6. Data were obtained for 1 payroll period during the year (primarily in early 1961) for all nonsupervisory employees (including working supervisors or foremen) in the offices and plants of establishments in the 6 broad industry divisions shown in Table 3. The scope of the survey excluded government institutions and the construction and extractive industries. The establishments within the scope of the survey were those employing 50 or more workers except in the largest areas, where the minimum size was 100 employees in manufacturing, public utilities, and retail trade.

7. One exception is employees of the Federal Government. Vacation provisions for the 1 million Government workers covered by the Federal Classification Act were reduced by the Annual and Sick Leave Act of 1951 from a uniform 26 days' annual leave to 13 days for employees with less than 3 years' service, 20 days for those with 3 but less than 15 years, and 26 days for those with 15 years or more.

8. "Vacations with Pay in Union Agreements, 1940," *Monthly Labor Review*, November, 1940, pp. 1070-77.

9. *Paid Vacation Provisions in Major Union Contracts, 1957* (BLS Bull. 1233, 1958); for summary, see *Monthly Labor Review*, July, 1958, pp. 744-51.

10. This figure is based on these computations:

a) To estimate the extent of the understatement because the survey week generally avoids all major holidays: The most recent survey week containing Labor Day (September, 1959) showed 600,000 more persons on vacation than in the following September. The last survey week containing July 4 (July, 1954) showed 1.3 million more people on vacation than in the following July. Assuming 7 holidays a year, 6 of which have the same effect as Labor Day, and adding 1.5 million for the seventh (July 4), additional vacation weeks due to the occurrence of holidays would be between 5 and 5½ million. Variations in the specific identity of the 6 paid holidays received by the average worker (footnote 15) due to differences in local customs, worker desires, employer practice, etc., account for the assumption that some workers observe holidays (and take vacations during the holiday week) on at least 7 different days during the year.

b) To estimate the extent of the understatement because no allowance was made for part-time vacations: According to household survey data, in the average week, about one-half of 1 per cent of all employed persons take about one-third week part-time vacation, For 1960, this amounted to approximately 4-5 million vacation weeks. However, certain part-week vacations may not be fully reported in the monthly survey (for example, in weeks containing a holiday that are not survey weeks). Consequently, a judgment was made that the total understatement for part-week vacations might be somewhat higher than these statistics would indicate.

11. Special Labor Force Report 14, *Labor Force and Employment in 1960* (Bureau of Labor Statistics, 1961), Table E-3, p. A-36.

12. "Vacations and Holiday Provisions in Union Agreements," *Monthly Labor Review*, May, 1943, p. 929.

13. "Paid Holidays in Major Contracts, 1958," *Monthly Labor Review*, January, 1959, pp. 26-32.

14. *Ibid.*, p. 30.

15. Estimates in the tabulation presented here were derived as follows:

Average hours of work: The drop of 1½ hours per week seems reasonable in view of the 1.3-hour drop for full-time workers between 1948 and 1960 (Table 1). Comparable estimates for 1940 are not available.

Paid vacation: Figure assumes an average paid vacation per employee of 0.3 week in 1940 and 1.5 weeks in 1960. The 1940 figure would make allowance for the following paid vacation: none for farm workers; 1 week for one-fourth of all manual and service workers (roughly the proportion of the 1940 survey for union members; see footnote 8); 2 weeks for one-half of the white-collar workers; and 1 week for one-fourth of the white-collar workers. The 1960 figure is based on 1.3 weeks of full vacation (Table 6) plus an allowance for the understatements described in footnote 10.

Paid holidays: Figure represents the difference between 2 paid holidays in 1940 and 6 paid holidays in 1960. The 1940 figure allows no paid holidays for farm workers, 1 for manual workers, and 5 for white-collar workers. The 1960 figure is based on 7.0-7.8 paid holidays for workers in metropolitan areas (Table 7) and a smaller number for workers outside these areas.

16. An alternative method of determining the allocation of productivity gains to income and leisure would be to compare the actual 1960 output with that resulting from applying 1960 man-hours at 1940 levels of productivity. This procedure also involves taking into account the reduced annual hours worked during this period. The results from the two methods are essentially the same.

Index

204